the hummingbird bakery

LIFE IS SWEET

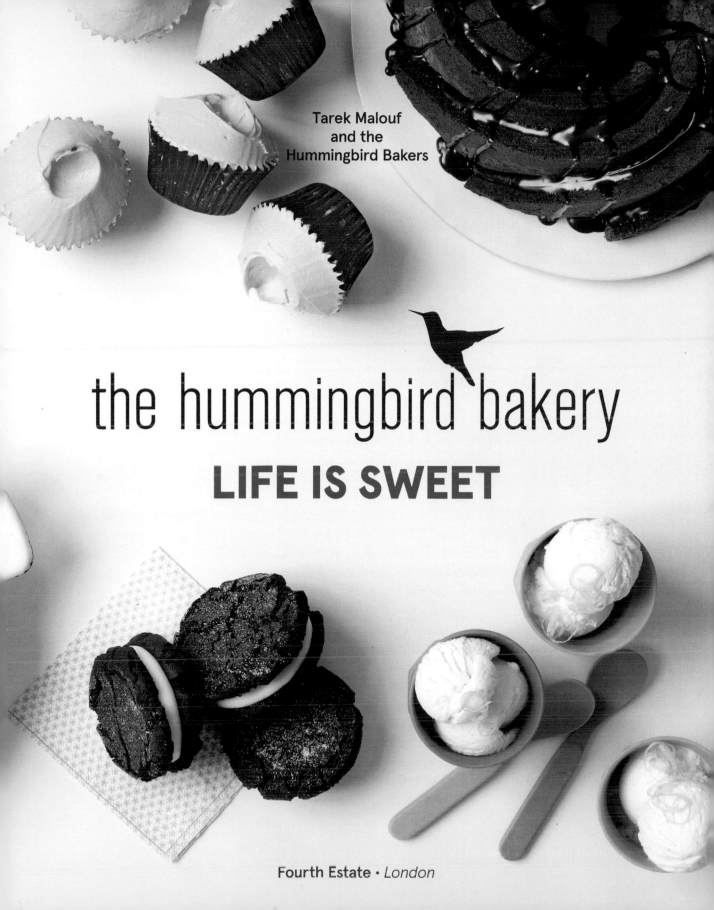

Tarek Malouf
and the
Hummingbird Bakers

the hummingbird bakery
LIFE IS SWEET

Fourth Estate · London

About the Author

It's hard to imagine that cupcakes and Red Velvet cake were virtually unknown in the UK before Tarek Malouf opened the first Hummingbird Bakery on London's Portobello Road in 2004. The Hummingbird Bakery has recently celebrated its tenth anniversary and has London-based bakeries in South Kensington, Soho, Spitalfields, Islington and Richmond, with three bakeries in Dubai. Since the very first day it opened its doors, everything at the Hummingbird Bakery has been baked fresh, with each site having its own kitchen and baking team, making sure the authentic American cakes and desserts taste as close to home-baked as possible.

Tarek grew up in London, attending the American School in London and later university in London and Los Angeles. While working for America's ABC News network, he noticed that the range of indulgent, high-quality cakes and bakes loved by Americans was almost non-existent in the UK. He decided it was time to bring these treats to the British public. After sampling more cakes than he should, and attending baking classes in New York in order to understand the different ingredients and techniques, the next step was to devise recipes and test them over and over on friends and family, and thus the Hummingbird Bakery was born. Tarek lives in London and *Life Is Sweet* is his fourth cookbook.

hummingbirdbakery.com

Contents

6   Introduction

8   **Cakes**

32   **Cupcakes**

58   **Layer Cakes**

90   **Pies**

118   **Cookies & Candies**

150   **Traybakes**

170   **Pancakes**

188   **Ice Cream**

210   **Puddings**

224   **Bread & Savouries**

246   Baking Essentials

252   Index

256   Acknowledgements

Introduction

When I opened the door of The Hummingbird Bakery in Portobello Road in 2004, and let the first customer in, I didn't realise that I was also opening the door onto a journey that would take me into the almost endless world of American baking. A handful of loyal customers accompanied me, at that first bakery, in discovering new American-style goodies. They were soon joined by many home-bakers, indulging their sweet tooths, honing their whisking and frosting skills, wowing their friends, colleagues and families with impressive multi-layer cakes, fluffy cupcakes and abundant sweet bakes. As more Hummingbird Bakery branches opened in London, our reach expanded much further thanks to our recipe books and social media pages. What we all share is a love of baking and an appreciation for the quirky fabulousness that is the American baked good!

Americana can be loud – all neon lights and shiny colours. There are those American goodies we're all familiar with: they stand out, demand to be noticed and they almost seem to know they're famous. But there's more to the United States and its sweet treats than that. Whilst every American region has its specialties, there's no place like the South if you want to enter a unique world of baked goods. These goodies will draw you in and envelop you like the sweet scent of a pie cooling in an open window.

Down south, things are slower and most definitely sweeter. When I started to think about what kind of recipes I wanted to gather and write for this book, my mind kept turning back to some of the tantalisingly special things that I had eaten on my trips to the United States and especially to the South. I knew that beyond the Pecan Pies and Red Velvet Cakes there were so many other recipes, unknown in the UK, that were begging to be discovered by our wonderful home-bakers.

I decided to go on a journey that would take me from New York City down to Durham in North Carolina, on to Atlanta and New Orleans, and end up in Dallas. Visiting relatives and old friends, I had come armed with only one demand: take me to the best desserts in town! And everyone duly helped out – after all, who could turn down the chance to eat dessert in the name of research?

In eating my way southwards, I discovered the rich, spicy tastes of old-fashioned recipes known only in specific regions; treats that were show stoppers; cakes that needed many steps and careful consideration (people had more time for baking in the past); but also easy recipes that could be mixed up in minutes but tasted just as good.

Running through all the recipes was a history of the South, and indeed the United States as a whole. Ginger, cinnamon and nutmeg from the Old World, liberally used, blending together with pecans and pumpkins from the New World. Fruits that need the hot sun, such as peaches from Georgia and oranges from Florida, to freshen things up and give a zing to cakes and pies. The peanuts and sweet potatoes used by African slaves in their daily cooking, along with cornbread and molasses, that influenced American baking in a unique way. Peanut butter in particular is so familiar to the American palate that it is strange to think it seemed crazily exotic to British bakers a generation ago. The Southern baker has never shied away from experimentation, with vintage recipes made with odd ingredients sitting alongside the traditional goodies made with the Holy Trinity of Southern ingredients: pumpkins, pecans and bourbon. Throw in a lot of chocolate, some marshmallows and maybe a little more bourbon and you're on your way to discovering how Southerners like their desserts!

Most of all, I am excited to introduce readers to recipes that they have probably not seen before. I know how excited they will be to progress that one step further into the rich history and techniques of American baking - to treat their friends and family with delicious creations. At The Hummingbird Bakery we love the fact that we've brought our readers on an American baking journey, and we're excited to say that we think we've reached the final destination. We're kicking back on the rocking chair with our plate of pie and declaring that Life is Sweet.

Tarek

Cakes

Gooey Butter Cake
Oatmeal Spice Cake
7Up Pound Cake
Black Fruitcake
Molasses Pecan Crumb Cake
Kentucky Bourbon Cake
Chocolate Bundt Cake
Ozark Pudding Cake
Gingerbread Cake
Tunnel of Fudge Cake
Upside-down Pear Cake

Gooey Butter Cake

**Makes one 23 x 32cm
(9 x 13in) cake, to slice
as desired**

For the cake
55ml (2fl oz) whole milk
55ml (2fl oz) water
50g (2oz) unsalted butter
2½ tsp dried active or
   instant yeast
265g (9½oz) plain flour
50g (2oz) caster sugar
½ tsp salt
1 large egg

For the gooey butter filling
310g (11oz) unsalted butter,
   softened
160ml (5½fl oz) condensed
   milk (sweetened)
160g (5½oz) golden syrup
2 large eggs
90g (3oz) plain flour
1½ tsp vanilla extract
Pinch of salt

Icing sugar, to decorate

One 23 x 32cm (9 x 13in) tin

This cake of two parts, a yeast dough base and soft, gooey topping, originates in St Louis, Missouri. Remember to take it out of the oven while still very slightly wobbly – it will firm up and set as it cools.

1. To make the cake, preheat the oven to 175°C (350°F), Gas mark 4. Grease the tin with butter and dust with flour.
2. Heal the milk, water and butter in a small saucepan over a low heat until the butter has melted. Allow to cool until lukewarm, sprinkle the yeast over the top and stir. Leave for 10 minutes.
3. Put the flour, sugar and salt in the bowl of a freestanding mixer or a bowl you can use an electric whisk in and mix together with a fork. Pour in the yeast mixture and egg and mix for 2 minutes at a medium speed, making sure you scrape down the sides of the bowl as you go, until combined. Switch to the dough hook and knead for 10 minutes on a medium speed.
4. Pour the dough into the prepared tin – it will be soft and sticky. Press the dough into the tin so that it fills it up completely, pressing it up the sides of the tin. Set aside while you make the filling. The dough will rise a little in the tin as you prepare the filling – this is normal.
5. Using a freestanding electric mixer with the paddle attachment or a hand-held electric whisk, beat the butter for around 5 minutes on a medium-high speed until light and fluffy. Add two-thirds of the condensed milk and beat on a medium-high speed until light. Add the syrup and mix thoroughly.
6. Add the eggs, one at a time, on a lower speed, mixing in between each addition, and then continue beating on a medium-high speed for about 2 minutes until the batter is light and fluffy. Mix in the flour and remaining condensed milk, a little at a time, alternating between the two ingredients. Add the vanilla and salt at the end and mix well.
7. Spoon and spread the filling over the yeast dough and bake for 30 minutes or until golden. The filling will be slightly wobbly, but it will set as it cools. Dust the cake with icing sugar once cool.

Oatmeal Spice Cake

Makes one 23 x 32cm (9 x 13in) cake, to slice as desired

For the spice cake
90g (3oz) rolled oats
290ml (10fl oz)
   boiling water
200g (7oz) plain flour
1½ tsp bicarbonate of soda
1½ tsp ground cinnamon
½ tsp salt
½ tsp ground nutmeg
115g (4oz) unsalted butter,
   softened
200g (7oz) soft light
   brown sugar
110g (4oz) caster sugar
2 large eggs
2 tbsp pure cane molasses,
   such as Meridian

For the coconut topping
55g (2oz) unsalted butter
200g (7oz) soft light
   brown sugar
120ml (4fl oz) whipping
   cream
100g (3½oz) shredded
   or desiccated coconut
120g (4oz) chopped pecans

One 23 x 32cm (9 x 13in) tin

A moist, spiced sponge, rich with molasses and brown sugar and topped with a lovely coconut and pecan crust. Be careful when finishing the crust under the hot grill – you want it bubbly and brown, but not burnt to a crisp!

1. To make the cake, preheat the oven to 175°C (350°F), Gas mark 4. Line the tin with non-stick baking parchment.
2. Mix the oats and boiling water together in a bowl and set aside. In a separate bowl, sift together the flour, bicarbonate of soda, cinnamon, salt and nutmeg.
3. Using a freestanding electric mixer with the paddle attachment or a hand-held electric whisk, cream the butter and sugars together for around 5 minutes on a medium-high speed until light and fluffy.
4. Add the eggs, one at a time, on a lower speed, scraping down the sides of the bowl after each addition. Add the molasses and mix until just incorporated. Next, add the dry ingredients on a low speed, making sure not to overbeat, until just incorporated and mixed through. Stir in the oats and water mixture by hand.
5. Pour the mixture into the prepared tin and bake for 30–35 minutes, until a skewer inserted into the cake comes out clean. Allow to cool in the tin for about an hour before you put the topping on.
6. To make the coconut topping, gently heat the butter, brown sugar and cream in a saucepan until the sugar is dissolved, and then take off the heat. Add the coconut and pecans and mix well.
7. Spread the topping over the cake and put under a hot grill for 2–3 minutes, until the topping is bubbly and browned. Do not step away from the grill – it can burn very easily.

7Up Pound Cake

Makes one 900g (2lb) loaf cake, to slice as desired

165g (6oz) unsalted butter
320g (11oz) caster sugar
3 large eggs
200g (7oz) plain flour
1 tsp grated lemon zest
½ tsp vanilla extract
90ml (3fl oz) (less than
   a third of a can)
   7Up or other lemon-lime
   carbonated drink

One 900g (2lb) loaf tin

Recipes using various carbonated soft drinks abound in vintage American recipe booklets. Most church groups and school parent-teacher associations still produce these spiral-bound booklets, with recipes donated by their members. This simple pound cake is made moist and slightly citrusy by using 7Up, but you can substitute your own favourite lemony fizzy drink.

1. Preheat the oven to 170°C (325°F), Gas mark 3. Line the loaf tin with non-stick baking parchment.
2. Using a freestanding electric mixer with the paddle attachment or a hand-held electric whisk, cream the butter and sugar together for around 10 minutes on a medium-high speed until very light and fluffy.
3. Add the eggs, one at a time, mixing after each addition, beating only until just incorporated. Remember to scrape down the sides of the bowl occasionally. Mix in the flour, lemon zest and vanilla extract until thoroughly mixed, but do not overbeat. Fold in the 7Up or equivalent by hand.
4. Spoon the mixture into the prepared tin and level the surface. Bake for about 1 hour or until a skewer inserted into the cake comes out clean and the top bounces back when lightly touched. Cool briefly in the tin and then transfer to a wire rack to cool completely.

Black Fruitcake

**Makes one 25cm (10in) ring
cake or two 900g (2lb) loaf
cakes, to slice as desired**

100g (3½oz) prunes,
   pitted and chopped
125g (4½oz) dates,
   pitted and chopped
100g (3½oz) currants
100g (3½oz) raisins
60g (2oz) each candied
   orange and lemon peel
60g (2oz) candied pineapple
75g (2½oz) glacé cherries,
   halved
300ml (10½fl oz) ruby port
160ml (5½fl oz) dark rum
270g (9½oz) plain flour
2 tsp bicarbonate of soda
1 tsp each ground allspice
and cinnamon
¾ tsp each ground
   nutmeg, mace and cloves
½ tsp salt
150g (5½oz) unsalted
   butter, softened
200g (7oz) dark muscovado
   sugar
3 large eggs
80g (3oz) pure cane
   molasses, such as Meridian
1½ tsp vanilla extract
115g (4oz) pecans or walnuts,
   coarsely chopped

*One 25cm (10in) ring mould
or two 900g (2lb) loaf tins*

We couldn't resist including this traditional Southern recipe,
rich with boozy fruits, molasses, dark sugar and spices. As with
all fruitcakes, if you make this a few months in advance and
season it with rum every few days, it'll be so much better.

1. In a large Tupperware or glass container with a lid, combine
the dried, candied and glacé fruits with 200ml (7fl oz) of the
port and all the rum and cover. This should be kept at room
temperature for at least 2 days – stirring twice a day. It can be
left for up to 6 weeks.
2. Preheat the oven to 150°C (300°F), Gas mark 2 and grease
the ring mould or loaf tins with butter.
3. In a large bowl, sift together the flour, bicarbonate of soda,
spices and salt.
4. Using a freestanding electric mixer with the paddle attachment
or a hand-held electric whisk, cream the butter and sugar together
for around 5 minutes on a medium-high speed until light and fluffy.
5. Add the eggs, one at a time, on a lower speed, scraping down
the sides of the bowl after each addition and beating well. Mix
in the molasses and vanilla on a low speed, and then add the dry
ingredients, a few tablespoons at a time. Stir in the fruit and nuts
by hand, with any leftover soaking liquid. The fruit and nuts and
liquid can be puréed if you prefer a more smooth-textured cake.
6. Scrape the batter into the prepared ring mould or loaf tins
and bake for 1 hour 30 minutes–1 hour 50 minutes, until a skewer
inserted into the cake comes out clean. Cool the cake in the tin,
then skewer little holes on top and pour in the remaining port.
You can also sprinkle with more dark rum if desired. Turn out the
cake once the extra liquid has soaked in and cool completely.
7. Wrap the cake tightly with baking parchment and foil and store
at room temperature for at least a week before eating. If fully
sealed, the cake can be stored for a further two to three months,
and 'seasoned' every few days with some more rum.

Molasses Pecan Crumb Cake

Makes one 23cm (9in) cake, to slice as desired

For the crumb topping
70g (2½oz) dark
  muscovado sugar
100g (3½oz) plain flour
55g (2oz) unsalted butter,
  cut into small cubes
50g (2oz) pecans,
  finely chopped

For the cake
200g (7oz) golden caster
  sugar
170g (6oz) unsalted butter,
  melted
175g (6oz) pure cane
  molasses, such as
  Meridian
2 tsp vanilla extract
2 large eggs
355g (12oz) plain flour
2 tsp ground ginger
1 tsp ground cinnamon
1 tsp ground allspice
1 tsp bicarbonate of soda
½ tsp salt
235ml (8fl oz) warm coffee
  (filter or instant)
75g (2½oz) pecans,
  chopped

*One 23cm (9in) deep
spring-form cake tin*

Molasses was historically imported into America from the Caribbean and continued to be the main form of sweetener until around World War I, as normal sugar was very expensive. Still commonly used in American baking, it makes things moist and rich and irresistible.

1. Base line the spring-form cake tin with non-stick baking parchment. Preheat the oven to 175°C (350°F), Gas mark 4.
2. To make the crumb topping, mix the muscovado sugar and flour in a bowl. With cold, dry fingers, rub the cubes of butter into the sugar and flour to make crumbs. With a fork, mix in the pecans. Put into the fridge while you make the cake.
3. Using a freestanding electric mixer with the paddle attachment or a hand-held electric whisk, mix together the sugar, butter, molasses and vanilla on a medium speed until very well mixed and smooth.
4. Add the eggs, one at a time, on a lower speed, scraping down the sides of the bowl after each addition. Sift together the flour, ginger, cinnamon, allspice, bicarbonate of soda and salt. Mix in the flour and spices and the coffee, alternating between the two, starting and finishing with the flour and spices. Add the pecans and mix in by hand.
5. Pour the batter (it will be thin) into the prepared spring-form tin. Sprinkle evenly with the crumb topping that has been chilling in the fridge.
6. Bake for about 50 minutes–1 hour until the top is firm and springy and a skewer inserted into the cake comes out clean. Best served warm after cooling for 30–45 minutes.

Kentucky Bourbon Cake

**Makes one 25cm
(10in) ring cake,
to slice as desired**

You don't have to use actual Kentucky bourbon for this cake – any whiskey will do, but bourbon does make it that extra bit authentic. Close your eyes after a few slices and you could actually be in the Bluegrass State!

For the cake

375g (13oz) plain flour
1 tsp baking powder
½ tsp bicarbonate of soda
1 tsp salt
225g (8oz) unsalted butter,
    softened
300g (10½oz) caster sugar
100g (3½oz) soft light
    brown sugar
4 large eggs
60ml (2fl oz) Kentucky
    bourbon or whiskey
235ml (8fl oz) buttermilk

For the glaze

85g (3oz) unsalted butter
150g (5½oz) caster sugar
60ml (2fl oz) Kentucky
    bourbon or whiskey

One 25cm (10in) ring mould

1. To make the cake, preheat the oven to 175°C (350°F), Gas mark 4. Grease the ring mould with butter and dust with flour and set aside.
2. In a bowl, sift together the flour, baking powder, bicarbonate of soda and salt. Set aside.
3. Using a freestanding electric mixer with the paddle attachment or a hand-held electric whisk, cream the butter and sugars together for around 5 minutes on a medium-high speed until light and fluffy.
4. Add the eggs, one at a time, on a lower speed, scraping down the sides of the bowl after each addition. In a small jug, mix together the bourbon and buttermilk by hand. Add the flour mixture to the bowl in three additions, alternating with the bourbon and buttermilk, adding the flour first. Only mix until the ingredients are just incorporated. Finish mixing in the last addition by hand.
5. Pour the batter into the prepared ring mould and bake for 40-45 minutes. When the cake is golden on top and bounces back when lightly touched, remove from the oven and leave in the mould.
6. To make the glaze, combine the butter, sugar and bourbon in a saucepan. Place over a low heat and cook just until the butter melts and the sugar is dissolved, then whisk vigorously to combine.
7. Take the cake, which should still be in the mould, and poke holes all over the top of the cake with a skewer. Pour three-quarters of the glaze slowly over the cake, letting it soak in carefully. Save the remaining quarter of the glaze.
8. Allow the cake to cool for 30 minutes, then flip over and turn out of the mould. Brush the remaining glaze over the top of the cake.

Chocolate Bundt Cake

Makes one 25cm (10in) Bundt cake, to slice as desired

For the cake
270g (9½oz) plain flour
1¼ tsp bicarbonate of soda
½ tsp baking powder
¼ tsp salt
295ml (10½fl oz) buttermilk
70g (2½oz) cocoa powder
235g (8oz) mayonnaise
2 large eggs
165g (6oz) soft light brown sugar
160g (5½oz) caster sugar
1½ tsp vanilla extract
60g (2oz) dark chocolate (minimum 70% cocoa solids), coarsely chopped

For the chocolate glaze
2 tbsp golden syrup
2 tbsp water
55g (2oz) caster sugar
85g (3oz) dark chocolate (minimum 70% cocoa solids)

One 25cm (10in) Bundt pan or ring mould

Yes, you read correctly, this cake contains mayonnaise! Many vintage American recipes substituted processed shortcuts for separate ingredients. In this extremely delicious chocolate cake, the oil or butter is replaced with mayonnaise – and before you panic, it works beautifully. American Bundt tins, which make for a prettier cake, can be ordered online and will last you for years.

1. To make the cake, preheat the oven to 175°C (350°F), Gas mark 4. Grease the Bundt pan or ring mould with butter and dust with flour and set aside.

2. In a bowl, sift together the flour, bicarbonate of soda, baking powder and salt. Set aside.

3. Using a freestanding electric mixer with the paddle attachment or a hand-held electric whisk, mix together the buttermilk, cocoa, mayonnaise, eggs, both sugars and vanilla. Mix until smooth. Fold in the dry ingredients and chocolate by hand and make sure everything is well mixed.

4. Pour and scrape the batter into the prepared mould and bake for 45–50 minutes. When the cake bounces back when lightly touched, remove from the oven and leave in the mould to cool for about 20 minutes, then turn out onto a wire rack to cool completely.

5. To make the glaze, put the syrup, water and sugar into a small pan over a low heat until the sugar has dissolved. Remove from the heat and allow to cool to warm. If you add the chocolate when the mixture is too hot, the chocolate will seize. Stir in the chocolate until it's smooth. Cool until slightly thickened and then spread or drizzle over the cake.

Ozark Pudding Cake

**Makes one 25cm (10in)
cake, to slice as desired**

2 large, ripe, firm apples
(such as Pink Lady),
peeled, cored and cut
into quarters
135g (5oz) plain flour
1 tsp baking powder
1 tsp ground ginger
½ tsp salt
60g (2oz) unsalted butter,
softened
200g (7oz) caster sugar,
plus 1 tsp for sprinkling
on top
1 large egg
1 tsp vanilla extract
55g (2oz) toasted flaked
almonds

*One 25cm (10in) cast-iron
skillet or ovenproof pan*

The Ozark Mountains are mostly in Missouri and Arkansas, and this baked-in-a-skillet cake was supposedly the favourite of President Harry S. Truman, a Missourian. If you want to experiment a little, use pears instead of the apples, but make sure you choose a firm-fleshed variety so that they don't turn too mushy when baked.

1. Preheat the oven to 175°C (350°F), Gas mark 4. Grease the bottom and sides of the skillet or ovenproof pan with butter.
2. Finely chop one of the apples. The other apple should be thinly sliced vertically. Sift together the flour, baking powder, ginger and salt into a bowl.
3. Using a freestanding electric mixer with the paddle attachment or a hand-held electric whisk, cream the butter and sugar together on a medium speed just until it resembles wet sand. Do not cream to light and fluffy.
4. Add the egg and vanilla and blend on a medium-high speed until light and fluffy. Turn down the speed to low and add the flour mixture in one addition. Mix until just blended – this batter will be stiff. Fold in the chopped apple and half the almonds and stir a couple of times by hand until just blended.
5. Drop the thick batter onto the prepared skillet or ovenproof pan and smooth down gently to make an even level. Arrange the apple slices on top of the batter – fanning out the slices around the centre. Sprinkle the remaining almonds and 1 teaspoon sugar over the top.
6. Bake in the oven for 35–40 minutes until the cake is golden in colour and bounces back gently when lightly touched. The cake will continue to cook in the skillet when removed from the oven, so be careful not to overcook. Serve warm on the day it is baked.

Gingerbread Cake

Makes one 23cm (9in) square cake, to slice as desired

225g (8oz) unsalted butter

120ml (4fl oz) water

175g (6oz) pure cane molasses, such as Meridian

175g (6oz) dark honey (chestnut or darker wildflower)

215g (7½oz) dark muscovado sugar

400g (14oz) plain flour

1½ tsp bicarbonate of soda

½ tsp salt

2 tsp ground ginger

2 tsp ground cinnamon

½ tsp allspice

¼ tsp ground cloves

3 large eggs

120ml (4fl oz) whole milk

1 tbsp grated fresh ginger

One 23cm (9in) square tin

This cake is seriously dense and rich. Using a combination of dark sugar, dark honey and molasses adds to the intensity and keeps the finished cake moist and slightly sticky. You can make it zingier by adding another tablespoon or two of freshly grated ginger. Eat plain or with some whipped cream to balance it out.

1. Preheat the oven to 170°C (325°F), Gas mark 3. Line the tin with non-stick baking parchment on the bottom and up the sides.
2. Place the butter, water, molasses, honey and muscovado sugar in a saucepan and put on a low heat. Stir frequently and cook until the butter has melted and everything is thoroughly mixed together – do not allow to boil. Remove from the heat and set aside to cool.
3. In a bowl, sift together the flour, bicarbonate of soda, salt and spices. Set aside.
4. When the molasses mixture has cooled enough so that it's just lukewarm transfer to a mixing bowl, add the eggs, one at a time, beating well after each addition. Add the milk and mix to combine well. Fold the dry ingredients into the batter. There may be some lumps, but don't worry as long as most of them have been mixed in. Don't vigorously mix. Finally, stir in the grated fresh ginger.
5. Bake in the oven for 1 hour–1 hour 15 minutes, or until the top bounces back when lightly touched and a skewer inserted into the cake comes out clean. Cool for at least 15 minutes in the tin before turning out onto a wire rack to cool completely. The cake can be served with whipped cream, if desired.

Tunnel of Fudge Cake

**Makes one 25cm (10in)
Bundt cake, to slice
as desired**

For the cake
390g (13½oz) unsalted
    butter, softened
375g (13oz) caster sugar
6 large eggs
250g (9oz) icing sugar,
    stirred to lighten
    and smooth out
305g (11oz) plain flour
90g (3oz) cocoa powder
1 tsp vanilla extract
250g (9oz) chopped
    walnuts

For the chocolate glaze
90g (3oz) icing sugar,
    sifted
30g (1oz) cocoa powder
4 tbsp warm milk

*One 25cm (10in) Bundt
pan or ring mould*

This recipe is adapted from the runner-up in the 1966 Pillsbury
Bake-Off. The original recipe used Pillsbury powdered mix and
became an instant hit after the company printed it in newspaper
ads. The cake will have a gooey middle, so don't test it with a skewer.
And use the nuts or it won't work!

1. To make the cake, preheat the oven to 170°C (325°F), Gas mark 3.
Grease the Bundt pan with butter and set aside.
2. Using a freestanding electric mixer with the paddle attachment
or a hand-held electric whisk, beat the butter and sugar for about
5 minutes on medium speed until light and creamy. Lower the speed
and add the eggs, one at a time, scraping down the sides of the bowl
after each addition and mixing until just incorporated. Gradually add
the icing sugar, mixing well. Add the flour, cocoa, vanilla and walnuts
and mix until just combined.
3. Scrape the batter into the Bundt pan and smooth the top. Bake
for 55–60 minutes. The cake will not be done in the centre, but
will be dry on top and separated slightly from the sides of the pan.
Remove from the oven and let stand in the pan on a wire rack for
1 hour. Loosen from the sides gently with a spatula after 1 hour and
allow to cool in the pan for a further hour. If you take the cake out
of the pan too early, it can fall apart. Remove from the pan by
inverting the cake onto the rack, then cool completely.
4. To make the glaze, combine the glaze ingredients in a small bowl
and beat with a whisk until smooth.
5. While the cake is still on a wire rack, place a sheet of greaseproof
paper or a large plate under the rack to catch the drips. Spoon
the glaze over the top of the cake, letting it drip down the sides.
Let stand to set the glaze, then transfer carefully to a cake plate
to serve.

Upside-down Pear Cake

**Makes one 23 x 32cm
(9 x 13in) cake, to slice
as desired**

For the caramelised pears

6 large, ripe pears, peeled,
  cored and quartered
  lengthways
3 tbsp fresh lemon juice
40g (1½oz) unsalted butter
80g (3oz) caster sugar
130ml (4½fl oz) Kentucky
  bourbon or whiskey

For the cake

195g (7oz) plain flour
1½ tbsp ground ginger
1½ tsp ground cinnamon
½ tsp ground cloves
½ tsp grated nutmeg
½ tsp salt
160g (5½oz) unsalted
  butter
75g (2½oz) dark muscovado
  sugar
4 large eggs
170g (6oz) pure cane
  molasses, such as
  Meridian
3 tbsp boiling water
1½ tsp bicarbonate
  of soda

One 23 x 32cm (9 x 13in) tin

We suppose you could use apples instead of pears, but pears work
so well with the sponge and look like jewels when you turn the cake
out on to your serving plate.

1. Preheat the oven to 175°C (350°F), Gas mark 4. Line the tin with
non-stick baking parchment.
2. To make the caramelised pears, mix the pears with the lemon
juice. In a large frying pan, melt the butter and sprinkle with half
the caster sugar. Put the pear quarters into the pan. Cook for about
5 minutes until brown on one side. Turn and cook for a further
5 minutes until the other side is brown. With a slotted spoon,
carefully remove the pear quarters and set aside to cool slightly.
3. Add the bourbon and the rest of the caster sugar to the pan
and cook and stir frequently for about 5 minutes until the mixture
becomes syrupy. Pour this syrup into the baking tin and tip the tin
to spread evenly over the bottom of the tin.
4. Start to arrange the pears from one corner so that they cover
the bottom of the tin and are facing the same way, with the tapered
ends lying in the same direction. Set aside.
5. To make the cake, sift together the flour, spices and salt in a bowl.
6. Using a freestanding electric mixer with the paddle attachment or
a hand-held electric whisk, cream the butter and sugar together for
around 5 minutes on a medium-high speed until light and fluffy. Add
the eggs, one at a time, on a lower speed, scraping down the sides
of the bowl after each addition. Only beat until just incorporated.
Add the molasses and beat for a few moments longer to mix.
7. In a small bowl, add the boiling water to the bicarbonate of soda
and set aside. Add half the flour mixture to the creamed mixture
on low speed. Then add the water and bicarbonate of soda and
the rest of the flour mixture and mix until well incorporated. It will
look like the mixture has split, but that is correct.
8. Scrape the mixture into the tin on top of the arranged pears and
bake for 25 minutes. Reduce the oven temperature to 165°C (325°F),
Gas mark 3 and bake for 10–15 minutes longer. The top should bounce
back when lightly touched. Cool in the tin for 1 hour, then run a knife
around the edges of the cake. Place a tray over the top of the tin and
carefully (but quickly) turn upside down.

Cupcakes

Grape Jelly Cupcakes
Blue Hawaiian Cupcakes
Bananas Foster Cupcakes
Pumpkin Chai Cupcakes
Tomato Soup Cupcakes
Pink Champagne Cupcakes
Toasted Marshmallow
    Cupcakes
Chocolate Chip 'Cupcakes'
Honey Cornbread Cupcakes
Mint Julep Cupcakes

Grape Jelly Cupcakes

Makes 12 cupcakes

For the cupcakes
2 large egg whites
60g (2oz) unsalted butter, softened
½ tsp salt
1 tsp vanilla extract
160g (5½oz) caster sugar
185g (6½oz) plain flour
1½ tsp baking powder
60ml (2fl oz) whole milk
60ml (2fl oz) water

For the filling
120ml (4fl oz) water
120ml (4fl oz) purple grape juice
3 tbsp cornflour
¼ tsp salt
110g (4oz) caster sugar
4 tbsp fresh lemon juice
30g (1oz) unsalted butter

For the frosting
1 large egg white
160g (5½oz) caster sugar
45ml (1½fl oz) purple grape juice

One 12-hole deep muffin tin, 12 paper muffin cases and two piping bags

Grape jelly in the USA is a seedless preserve or jam made from Concord grapes. This is hard to find in the UK, but using a purple grape juice will simulate the flavour.

1. To make the cupcakes, preheat the oven to 175°C (350°F), Gas mark 4, and line the muffin tin with the paper muffin cases.
2. Using a freestanding electric mixer with the whisk attachment or a hand-held electric whisk, whisk the egg whites until stiff. Set aside.
3. Again, using the mixer with the paddle attachment or a hand-held electric whisk, cream the butter, salt, vanilla and sugar together for around 5 minutes on a medium-high speed until light and fluffy.
4. Sift together the flour and baking powder into a bowl and add to the creamed mixture a third at a time, alternating with the milk and water. Scrape down the sides of the bowl after each addition and mix until smooth. Fold in the beaten egg whites by hand.
5. Scoop the mixture into the paper cases until three-quarters full. Bake for 20 minutes, or until the cupcakes are golden brown and bounce back when lightly touched. Leave to cool slightly before removing from the tin and placing on a wire rack to cool completely before frosting.
6. Whilst the cakes are baking, make the filling. Heat the water and grape juice in a saucepan on medium-low heat. Do not allow to boil. Combine the cornflour, salt and sugar in a small bowl and add to the grape juice and water. Cook over a low heat, whisking all the time, until thick. Once thick, add the lemon juice and butter and whisk briskly until well blended. Allow to cool completely.
7. To make the frosting, mix all the ingredients together in a small heatproof mixing bowl. Put the bowl over a pan of simmering water and beat with an electric whisk for 8–10 minutes until the mixture holds a peak. Remove from the heat and continue beating until the mixture is thick enough to spread.
8. Once the cupcakes are completely cool, use a sharp knife to make a hollow in the centre of each, approximately 2cm (¾in) in diameter and 3cm (1¼in) deep. Retain the cut-out piece of sponge.
9. Spoon the filling mix into a piping bag and fill the hollows in the cupcakes, then pop on the removed top. Pipe any extra filling on top.
10. Put the frosting into another piping bag with a nozzle of your choice and pipe it in a spiral motion, making sure you cover all the sponge. Repeat until all your cakes are complete.

Blue Hawaiian Cupcakes

Makes 12 cupcakes

For the cupcakes
425g (15oz) tin pineapple
    rings, in juice
2 tbsp water
215g (7½oz) caster sugar,
    plus 2 tbsp extra
2 tbsp fresh lemon juice
2 tbsp fresh lime juice
1 tsp vanilla extract
40ml (1½fl oz) dark rum
90g (3oz) unsalted butter,
    softened
2 large eggs
170g (6oz) plain flour
1½ tsp baking powder
¼ tsp salt
1½ tbsp Blue Curaçao
    (or Triple Sec, Cointreau
    or Grand Marnier)
Few drops of blue liquid
    food colouring (optional)

For the pineapple sauce
115g (4oz) unsalted butter
70g (2½oz) soft light brown
    sugar
45ml (1½fl oz) dark rum

**For the whipped cream
topping**
300ml (10½fl oz) double
    cream
100ml (3½fl oz) whipping
    cream
70g (2½oz) caster sugar
30ml (1fl oz) dark rum

When we're not drinking kitschy Blue Hawaiian cocktails from a big plastic pineapple-shaped cup (complete with paper cocktail umbrellas!), we're baking and eating them in boozy cupcake form. You can use any orange-based liqueur such as Triple Sec, Cointreau or Grand Marnier if you don't have or can't find Blue Curaçao.

1. To make the cupcakes, preheat the oven to 175°C (350°F), Gas mark 4. Grease the sides and bottoms of the muffin tin or ramekins with butter – do not put paper cases in.

2. Over a bowl, drain the pineapple rings, reserving 60ml (2fl oz) of the juice (you can discard the rest). Set the reserved juice aside. Trim the pineapple rings so that they will fit in the bottom of your muffin tin holes or your ramekins. Chop up the discarded pineapple finely, put into a bowl and set aside.

3. In a saucepan, heat the 2 tablespoons water with the 2 tablespoons sugar, just until the sugar dissolves. Take off the heat and then add the lemon and lime juices. Measure out about 70ml (2½fl oz) of the resulting sweet and sour mix into a bowl. To this add the vanilla extract, dark rum and reserved pineapple juice.

4. Using a freestanding electric mixer with the paddle attachment or a hand-held electric whisk, cream the butter and caster sugar together for around 5 minutes on a medium-high speed until light and fluffy.

5. Add the eggs, one at a time, on a lower speed, scraping down the bowl after each addition. Add the sweet and sour rum liquid and mix. Sift together the flour, baking powder and salt and mix into the wet ingredients on a low speed in one slow but steady addition. Don't overbeat. By hand, stir in the reserved pineapple pieces, Blue Curaçao and food colouring, if using.

6. To make the pineapple sauce, heat the butter and brown sugar in a small saucepan for around 3 minutes on a medium-low heat until the butter is melted and all is dissolved. Remove from the heat and stir in the rum.

7. To assemble the cupcakes, spoon about 1 teaspoon of the sauce on top of each pineapple ring. Spoon the batter in until each hole or ramekin is about three-quarters full. Using a 50ml (1¾ fl oz) ice-cream scoop can make this process easier and will result in even cupcakes.

For the decoration

40g (1½oz) desiccated
   coconut
12 maraschino cherries

*One 12-hole deep muffin
tin or 12 ramekins*

8. Bake the cupcakes for 25 minutes, or until the sponge bounces back when lightly touched. When they're done, allow to cool in the tin or ramekins for 10 minutes, then flip over carefully. It's best to take a tray and flip over the muffin tin all at once. The pineapple rings can be rearranged if they fall out or are dislodged to make them fit back on top of the cakes. Leave to cool completely.

9. To make the whipped cream topping, use a freestanding electric mixer with the whisk attachment or a hand-held electric whisk to whip the creams and sugar together until it starts to thicken and forms firm peaks. Fold in the rum carefully by hand.

10. Lightly toast the coconut until it is a light golden brown – this takes about 5–6 minutes in a hot oven, but keep checking as it will turn brown quite quickly. Top each cupcake with a dollop of the whipped cream, a maraschino cherry and a sprinkle of the toasted coconut. Paper cocktail umbrella is optional.

Bananas Foster Cupcakes

Makes 18 cupcakes

For the cupcakes
25g (1oz) piece fresh ginger,
   peeled and roughly sliced
115ml (4fl oz) water
195g (7oz) mashed ripe
   bananas
60ml (2fl oz) dark rum
90g (3oz) unsalted butter,
   softened
80ml (3fl oz) treacle
150g (5½oz) dark
   muscovado sugar
1 large egg
270g (9½oz) plain flour
2 tsp baking powder
1 tsp bicarbonate of soda
½ tsp salt
2 tsp ground ginger
1 tsp ground cinnamon
1 tsp ground nutmeg

For the sauce
75g (2½oz) dark muscovado
   sugar
45g (1½oz) unsalted butter
25ml (1fl oz) golden syrup
25ml (1fl oz) dark rum
25ml (1fl oz) crème de
   banane (optional –
   if not using, use
   50ml dark rum)

Bananas Foster is a dessert created in 1951 at Brennan's Restaurant in New Orleans. Bananas cooked in brown sugar, rum, butter, cinnamon and banana liqueur are then spectacularly flambéed at your table and served with vanilla ice cream, and here we present them to you in cupcake form. Dark sugar and treacle give the sponge a kick, and don't worry if you don't have any Crème de Banane – more rum will do!

1. To make the cupcakes, preheat the oven to 175°C (350°F), Gas mark 4, and line the muffin tins with the paper muffin cases.
2. In a saucepan, combine the ginger and water and bring to the boil. As soon as it boils, take off the heat and leave to steep for 30 minutes. Discard the ginger, straining through a sieve if necessary. Stir the banana and rum into the gingery water and set aside.
3. Using a freestanding electric mixer with the paddle attachment or a hand-held electric whisk, cream the butter, treacle and sugar together for around 5 minutes on a medium-high speed until light and creamy. Beat in the egg, on a lower speed, scraping down the sides of the bowl as you go. In a large bowl, sift together the flour, baking powder, bicarbonate of soda, salt, ginger, cinnamon and nutmeg. Add the dry ingredients and the banana mixture to the creamed mixture in alternate additions, being careful not to overmix.
4. Scoop into the paper cases until three-quarters full. Using a 50ml (1¾fl oz) ice-cream scoop can make this process easier and will result in even cupcakes. Bake for 15–20 minutes, or until the cupcakes bounce back when lightly touched. Leave to cool slightly before removing from the tin and placing on a wire rack to cool completely before frosting.
5. To make the sauce, combine the muscovado sugar, butter and syrup in a saucepan over a low heat and stir until they reach a simmer. Add the rum and crème de banane, if using, and cook for a further 2–3 minutes. Remove from the heat and set aside.
6. To make the frosting, mash the bananas in a small bowl with the lemon juice. Using a freestanding electric mixer with the paddle attachment or a hand-held electric whisk, beat the butter for a minute or two to loosen. Add the mashed banana and beat for 1–2 more minutes until well mixed. Add the icing sugar, a third at

For the frosting

130g (4½oz) mashed
　ripe bananas
1 tsp fresh lemon juice
225g (8oz) unsalted butter,
　softened
600g (1lb 5oz) icing sugar
25g (1oz) dark muscovado
　sugar
1 tsp ground cinnamon
1 tbsp dark rum
1 tsp vanilla extract

Two 12-hole deep muffin
tins and 18 paper muffin
cases

a time, on a low speed, then add the brown sugar, cinnamon, rum and vanilla. Turn the mixer up to medium and beat for an additional 5 minutes until light and fluffy.

7. To assemble the cupcakes, skewer each one three or four times and pour enough sauce into the holes so that they are quite soaked through. Allow the cupcakes and sauce to cool completely. This is very important, as the frosting will melt if the cupcake is even slightly warm.

8. Pipe or spoon generous amounts of the frosting onto each cupcake, gently smoothing over with a palette knife or spoon and making a nice swirl of frosting on each one.

Pumpkin Chai Cupcakes

Makes 12 cupcakes

For the cupcakes
135g (5oz) plain flour
1 tsp bicarbonate of soda
½ tsp salt
1 tsp ground cinnamon
½ tsp ground ginger
¼ tsp ground nutmeg
160g (5½oz) caster sugar
50g (1¾oz) soft light
  brown sugar
115ml (4fl oz) rapeseed
  or other flavourless
  vegetable oil
2 large eggs
210g (7½oz) tinned
  pumpkin purée
  (such as Libby's)

For the frosting
75ml (2½fl oz) water
65g (2oz) caster sugar
2 good-quality chai tea
  bags (such as Teapigs)
3 cardamom pods
2 whole cloves
1 cinnamon stick
115g (4oz) unsalted butter,
  softened
250g (9oz) full-fat
  cream cheese, such
  as Philadelphia, cold
100g (3½oz) icing sugar
½ tsp vanilla extract
1 tsp honey

*One 12-hole deep muffin tin
and 12 paper muffin cases*

Pumpkin spice means that autumn is on the way, Hallowe'en and Thanksgiving are on the horizon, and while it may not get too freezing cold down South, summer is definitely over. America's favourite autumn flavours work perfectly when transformed into cupcakes.

1. To make the cupcakes, preheat the oven to 175°C (350°F), Gas mark 4, and line the muffin tin with the paper muffin cases.
2. In a large bowl, sift together the flour, bicarbonate of soda, salt, cinnamon, ginger and nutmeg.
3. Using a freestanding electric mixer with the paddle attachment or a hand-held electric whisk, mix together the sugars and oil on a low speed until all combined and lighter in colour. Add the eggs, one at a time, on a low speed, scraping down the sides of the bowl after each addition, then add the pumpkin purée. Now add the dry ingredients to the mixture, folding them in carefully so that the mixture remains light.
4. Spoon the mixture into the paper cases until three-quarters full. Bake for 20 minutes, or until the cupcakes bounce back when lightly touched. Leave to cool slightly before removing from the tin and placing on a wire rack to cool completely before frosting.
5. To make the frosting, mix the water, sugar, tea bags, cardamom, cloves and cinnamon together in a saucepan and bring to the boil over a medium heat until the sugar dissolves. Lower the heat and simmer gently for a further 5–8 minutes. Take off the heat, strain the syrup into a clean bowl, squeezing the tea bags to get all the flavour out, and leave to cool completely.
6. Using a freestanding electric mixer with the paddle attachment or a hand-held electric whisk, beat the butter to loosen it up, then add the cream cheese and icing sugar on a low speed until incorporated. Turn the mixer to a high speed and beat for about 3 minutes until light and fluffy. Don't overbeat, or the cream cheese will split and become runny. Lower the speed and add the vanilla extract, honey and chai syrup until all are well combined. As soon as the frosting is combined, put into the fridge for about 2 hours so that the spicy flavours can intensify further.
7. Pipe or spoon generous amounts of the frosting onto each cupcake, gently smoothing over with a palette knife and making a nice swirl of frosting on each one

Tomato Soup Cupcakes

Makes 18 cupcakes

For the cupcakes
115g (4oz) unsalted butter,
   softened
285g (10oz) caster sugar
2 large eggs
270g (9½oz) plain flour
2 tsp baking powder
1 tsp bicarbonate of soda
1½ tsp ground allspice
1 tsp ground cinnamon
½ tsp ground cloves
60ml (2fl oz) water
295g (10½oz) tin
   condensed cream
   of tomato soup

For the frosting
100g (3½oz) unsalted
   butter, softened
240g (8½oz) full-fat
   cream cheese, such
   as Philadelphia, cold
400g (14oz) icing sugar
Ground cinnamon,
   to sprinkle

*Two 12-hole deep muffin
tins and 18 paper muffin
cases*

For that authentic American taste, use a can of Campbell's Cream of Tomato soup for this recipe. These cupcakes are most definitely sweet, and have a kind of carrot-cake flavour to them. Another vintage recipe that uses a non-conventional ingredient to perfection.

1. To make the cupcakes, preheat the oven to 175°C (350°F), Gas mark 4, and line the muffin tins with the paper muffin cases.
2. Using a freestanding electric mixer with the paddle attachment or a hand-held electric whisk, cream the butter and sugar together for around 5 minutes on a medium-high speed until light and fluffy.
3. Add the eggs, one at a time, on a lower speed, scraping down the sides of the bowl after each addition. Combine the flour, baking powder, bicarbonate of soda, allspice, cinnamon and cloves in a bowl and mix into the wet ingredients on a low speed in one slow but steady addition. Don't overbeat. Finally, add the water and condensed soup to make a thick batter.
4. Spoon the mixture into the paper cases until three-quarters full. Using a 50ml (1¾fl oz) ice-cream scoop can make this process easier and will result in even cupcakes. Bake for 20 minutes, or until a skewer inserted into a cupcake comes out clean. Leave to cool slightly before removing from the tin and placing on a wire rack to cool completely before frosting.
5. To make the frosting, using a freestanding electric mixer with the paddle attachment or a hand-held electric whisk, beat the butter to loosen it up, then add the cream cheese and icing sugar on a low speed until incorporated. Turn the mixer to a high speed and beat for about 3 minutes until light and fluffy. Don't overbeat or the cream cheese will split and become runny.
6. Pipe or spoon generous amounts of the frosting onto each cupcake, gently smoothing over with a palette knife and making a nice swirl of frosting on each one. Sprinkle the decorated cakes with cinnamon.

Pink Champagne Cupcakes

Makes 12 cupcakes

For the cupcakes
160g (5½oz) plain flour
1 tsp baking powder
½ tsp bicarbonate of soda
¼ tsp salt
2 large eggs
1 tsp vanilla extract
175g (6oz) caster sugar
115ml (4fl oz) rapeseed
   oil, or other flavourless
   vegetable oil
115ml (4fl oz) pink
   Champagne or pink
   sparkling wine

For the custard
350ml (12fl oz) single cream
4 large egg yolks
100g (3½oz) caster sugar
80ml (3fl oz) pink
   Champagne or pink
   sparkling wine
30g (1oz) cornflour
Up to ¼ tsp red food
   colouring gel (to make
   the custard the desired
   pink colour)
30g (1oz) unsalted butter
2 tsp vanilla extract

For the frosting
300ml (10½fl oz) double
   cream
40g (1½oz) caster sugar

*One 12-hole deep muffin
tin, 12 paper muffin cases
and a piping bag*

Now you don't have to break the bank and use actual champagne. Any pink or plain sparkling wine will do. These have a very subtle wine taste, and the fluffy sponge and luscious custard mean that one cupcake will not be enough.

1. To make the cupcakes, preheat the oven to 175°C (350°F), Gas mark 4, and line the muffin tin with the paper muffin cases.
2. In a large bowl, sift together the flour, baking powder, bicarbonate of soda and salt. Set aside.
3. Using a freestanding electric mixer with the paddle attachment or a hand-held electric whisk, beat together the eggs, vanilla and sugar for 2 minutes on a medium speed. Pour in the oil in a slow but steady stream until all is well incorporated. Add the flour mixture and Champagne in several additions, alternating between the two – flour first and last. Do not overbeat. Use a spatula to scrape down the sides of the bowl and ensure everything is combined.
4. Spoon the mixture into the paper cases until three-quarters full. Using a 50ml (1¾fl oz) ice-cream scoop can make this process easier and will result in even cupcakes. Bake for 15–20 minutes until the cupcakes bounce back when lightly touched. Leave to cool slightly before removing from the tin and placing on a wire rack to cool completely before filling and frosting.
5. To make the custard, heat the cream in a saucepan until it is hot, but don't let it boil. Meanwhile, whisk the egg yolks and sugar together in a bowl. Mix in the Champagne, and then the cornflour.
6. Add a quarter of the hot cream to the egg mixture, whisking vigorously so that the egg doesn't cook, but just warms up. Pour into the pan with the rest of the hot cream and cook over a medium-low heat, whisking constantly until the mixture starts to get thicker and bubbles. Once the mixture has bubbled for 1–2 minutes, take it off the heat. If necessary, you may have to strain it through a fine sieve to get any lumps out. If it splits at any stage, take it off the heat and use a hand-held blender to whizz it back together.
7. Put the custard into another bowl and mix through the red colouring, butter and vanilla until the butter melts and everything is well mixed. Cover with cling film, pressing it directly onto the surface to prevent a skin forming, and put into the fridge until cold.

8. To make the frosting, in the bowl of a freestanding electric mixer with the whisk attachment or using a hand-held electric whisk, whip the cream on medium speed. When the cream starts to thicken, but before it's whipped, add the sugar. Increase the speed and whip until it just starts to form peaks. Don't overwhip or it will get too hard or split.

9. Take 100g (3½oz) of the cool custard. If the custard is very stiff, beat briefly with a spatula until smooth. Then fold into the cream and put the frosting in the fridge.

10. Once the cupcakes are completely cool, use a sharp knife and remove a piece of sponge to make a hollow in the centre of each

▼

cupcake, approximately 2cm (¾in) in diameter and about 3cm (1¼in) deep. Retain the cut-out piece of sponge.

11. Spoon the custard into a piping bag and fill the hollows in the cupcakes, then pop the removed piece of sponge back on the cakes. If, once you've done all the cupcakes, there is custard left over, you can spread it thinly over the top of each one, making sure not to go over the edges.

12. Finally, pipe or spoon generous amounts of the frosting onto each cupcake, gently smoothing over with a palette knife and making a nice swirl of frosting on each one.

Toasted Marshmallow Cupcakes

Makes 12 cupcakes

For the cupcakes

300g (10½oz) sweet
  potatoes
115g (4oz) unsalted butter,
  softened
140g (5oz) soft light brown
  sugar
2 large eggs
3 tbsp maple syrup
½ tsp vanilla extract
135g (5oz) plain flour
1 tsp baking powder
¼ tsp bicarbonate of soda
Pinch of salt
½ tsp ground cinnamon
½ tsp ground nutmeg

For the frosting

70g (2½oz) caster sugar
¼ tsp cream of tartar
Pinch of salt
2 large egg whites
3 tbsp cold water
1 tsp vanilla extract
50g (1¾oz) marshmallow
  fluff

*One 12-hole deep muffin
tin, 12 paper muffin cases
and a cook's blowtorch*

In America sweet potatoes are known as yams, and baked in the oven with sugar, spices and marshmallows they are a typical Thanksgiving side dish. Careful when using the cook's blowtorch!

1. Preheat the oven to 200°C (400°F), Gas mark 6.

2. Wrap the sweet potatoes in foil and bake for about 45–60 minutes until tender. Once cooled, scoop out the flesh and mash.

3. To make the cupcakes, reduce the oven temperature to 175°C (350°F), Gas mark 4, and line the muffin tin with the paper cases.

4. Using a freestanding electric mixer with the paddle attachment or a hand-held electric whisk, cream the butter and sugar together for around 5 minutes on a medium-high speed until light and fluffy.

5. Add the eggs, one at a time, on a lower speed, scraping down the sides of the bowl after each addition. Then add the sweet potato flesh, maple syrup and vanilla and mix for a few moments until thoroughly incorporated. In a large bowl, sift together the flour, baking powder, bicarbonate of soda, salt, cinnamon and nutmeg. Lower the mixer speed and mix in the dry ingredients in one slow but steady addition. Don't overbeat.

6. Scoop the mixture into the paper cases until three-quarters full. Using a 50ml (1¾fl oz) ice-cream scoop can make this process easier and will result in even cupcakes. Bake for 15–20 minutes or until the cupcakes bounce back when lightly touched. Leave to cool slightly before removing from the tin and placing on a wire rack to cool completely before frosting.

7. To make the frosting, mix the caster sugar, cream of tartar, pinch of salt, egg whites and cold water together in a small heatproof mixing bowl. Put the bowl over a pan of simmering water and beat with an electric whisk for 5–7 minutes until the mixture is very hot to the touch and stiff peaks have formed. Remove the bowl from the heat and beat for 1 minute more. Add the vanilla extract and marshmallow fluff and beat until combined.

8. Pipe or spoon generous amounts of the frosting onto each cupcake, gently smoothing over with a palette knife or spoon and making a nice swirl of frosting on each one.

9. Using a cook's blowtorch, carefully torch the tops to brown them, avoiding the paper cases with the flame.

Chocolate Chip 'Cupcakes'

Makes 12 cupcakes

For the cupcakes
115g (4oz) unsalted butter,
  softened
80g (3oz) caster sugar
75g (2½oz) soft light
  brown sugar
½ tsp vanilla extract
1 large egg
150g (5½oz) plain flour
½ tsp bicarbonate of soda
½ tsp salt

For the topping
100g (3½oz) soft light
  brown sugar
1 large egg
Pinch of salt
170g (6oz) dark chocolate
  chips (minimum
  70% cocoa solids)
60g (2oz) chopped pecans
  (or walnuts)
½ tsp vanilla extract

*One 12-hole deep muffin tin
and 12 paper muffin cases*

These are a sort of chocolate chip cookie in a cupcake case. The texture is definitely not supposed to be cake-like, so don't worry when they come out dense and chewy. We'd suggest eating them on the day of baking or soon after.

1. To make the cupcakes, preheat the oven to 175°C (350°F), Gas mark 4, and line the muffin tin with the paper muffin cases.
2. Using a freestanding electric mixer with the paddle attachment or a hand-held electric whisk, cream the butter, sugars and vanilla together for around 5 minutes on a medium-high speed until light and fluffy. Beat in the egg, on a lower speed, scraping down the sides of the bowl as you go. In a separate bowl, sift together the flour, bicarbonate of soda and salt and mix into the wet ingredients on a low speed in one slow but steady addition. Don't overbeat. The cake mix will be quite stiff — more like a dough.
3. Use a tablespoon to form the mixture into twelve balls (roughly weighing 35g/1¼oz each). Place each one in a paper case and bake in the oven for 10 minutes. Meanwhile, prepare the topping.
4. Using a freestanding electric mixer with the paddle attachment or a hand-held electric whisk, beat the sugar, egg and salt for 3–4 minutes until thick and lighter in colour. Stir in the chocolate chips, pecans and vanilla extract by hand.
5. Take the cupcakes out of the oven and spoon one tablespoon of the topping over the partially baked cupcakes. Immediately put them back into the oven and cook for 12 minutes longer. These cupcakes come out as halfway between a cake and a cookie, so not as light and airy as normal cupcakes. Leave to cool slightly before removing from the tin and placing on a wire rack to cool completely.

Honey Cornbread Cupcakes

Makes 12 cupcakes

For the cupcakes
170g (6oz) yellow cornmeal
  (polenta)
135g (5oz) plain flour
1 tbsp baking powder
1 tsp ground cinnamon
½ tsp ground nutmeg
110g (4oz) caster sugar
1 tsp salt
2 large eggs
235ml (8fl oz) whole milk
115g (4oz) unsalted butter,
  melted
60g (2oz) runny honey

For the frosting
340g (12oz) unsalted
  butter, softened
75g (2½oz) runny honey
285g (10oz) icing sugar
150g (5½oz) full-fat
  cream cheese, such
  as Philadelphia, cold

*One 12-hole deep muffin tin
and 12 paper muffin cases*

Using cornmeal to make cornbread was something the early European settlers in America learned from the Native Americans they encountered. These cupcakes are sweet, denser than our normal sponges, and have a tangy cream cheese frosting flavoured with honey.

1. To make the cupcakes, preheat the oven to 175°C (350°F), Gas mark 4, and line the muffin tin with the paper muffin cases.
2. In a large bowl, mix the cornmeal, flour, baking powder, cinnamon, nutmeg, sugar and salt together thoroughly.
3. Using a freestanding electric mixer with the whisk attachment or a hand-held electric whisk, whisk the eggs, milk, melted butter and honey together on a medium speed until very well combined. Add the dry ingredients on a low speed in one slow but steady addition. Mix thoroughly but don't overbeat.
4. Carefully scoop the mixture into the paper cases until three-quarters full. Using a 50ml (1¾fl oz) ice-cream scoop can make this process easier and will result in even cupcakes. Bake for 20 minutes, or until the cupcakes bounce back when lightly touched. Leave to cool slightly before removing from the tin and placing on a wire rack to cool completely before frosting.
5. To make the frosting, in the bowl of a freestanding electric mixer with the paddle attachment or using a hand-held electric whisk, beat the butter for a minute to loosen it up, then add the honey and beat for a minute. Slowly add the icing sugar on a low speed until incorporated and beat for 2–3 minutes until light and fluffy. Add the cream cheese and mix briefly until incorporated – don't overbeat or it will split and become runny.
6. Pipe or spoon generous amounts of the frosting onto each cupcake, gently smoothing over with a palette knife or spoon and making a nice swirl of frosting on each one.

Mint Julep Cupcakes

Makes 12 cupcakes

**For the crystallised mint
leaf decoration (optional)**
1 egg white
Bowl of caster sugar
15–30 fresh mint leaves

For the cupcakes
115g (4oz) unsalted butter,
 softened
200g (7oz) caster sugar
2 large eggs
½ tsp vanilla extract
¼ tsp pure mint extract
115ml (4fl oz) whole milk
85ml (3fl oz) Kentucky
 bourbon or whiskey
185g (6½oz) plain flour
1½ tsp baking powder
½ tsp salt

For the frosting
175g (6oz) unsalted butter,
 softened
375g (13oz) icing sugar
40ml (1½fl oz) whole milk
¼ tsp pure mint extract
1 tbsp Kentucky bourbon
 or whiskey

*One 12-hole deep muffin tin
and 12 paper muffin cases*

The mint julep is a drink that Scarlett O'Hara would have offered
to one of her guests, made with sugar, mint and bourbon whiskey.
As with all our recipes calling for bourbon, you can use any whiskey
you have to hand.

1. To crystallise the mint leaves, whisk the egg white in a bowl until
frothy. In a second bowl, put a generous amount of caster sugar.
Dip the mint leaves gently into the frothy egg white so that they're
completely covered, then roll and press into the caster sugar.
Be sure to turn and press each side so both sides are covered.
2. Place the leaves on a tray lined with baking parchment and
allow to dry overnight before using as a decoration.
3. To make the cupcakes, preheat the oven to 175°C (350°F),
Gas mark 4, and line the muffin tins with the paper muffin cases.
4. Using a freestanding electric mixer with the paddle attachment
or a hand-held electric whisk, cream the butter and sugar together
for around 5 minutes on a medium-high speed until light and fluffy.
Add the eggs, one at a time, on a lower speed, scraping down the
sides of the bowl after each addition.
5. In a large jug, mix the vanilla, mint extract, milk and bourbon together
by hand. Sift together the flour, baking powder and salt. With the mixer
on a low speed, add the dry ingredients and the milk and bourbon
mixture in alternate additions, starting and ending with the dry.
6. Scoop into the paper cases until three-quarters full. Using a
50ml (1¾fl oz) ice-cream scoop can make this process easier and
will result in even cupcakes. Bake for 20–25 minutes, or until the
cupcakes are golden brown and bounce back when lightly touched.
Leave to cool slightly before removing from the tin and placing on
a wire rack to cool completely before frosting.
7. To make the frosting, in the bowl of a freestanding electric mixer
with the paddle attachment or using a hand-held electric whisk,
beat the butter for a minute to loosen it up, add the sugar gradually
on a lower speed, then turn to high and beat well. Add the milk
1 tablespoon at a time until the frosting is nice and soft and fluffy.
Finally, stir in the mint and bourbon.
8. Pipe or spoon generous amounts of the frosting onto each
cupcake, gently smoothing over with a palette knife or spoon and
making a nice swirl of frosting on each one, then place one or two
crystallised mint leaves on top.

Layer Cakes

Peanut Butter and Jelly Cake
Chocolate Doberge Cake
Lady Baltimore Cake
Gingerbread Icebox Cake
German Chocolate Cake
Lemon Doberge Cake
Alabama Little Layer Cake
Orange Layer Cake
Red Velvet Crepe Cake
Appalachian Stack Cake

Peanut Butter and Jelly Cake

Makes one 20cm (8in) cake, to slice as desired

For the cake

110g (4oz) unsalted butter, softened
380g (13oz) caster sugar
320g (11oz) plain flour
2 tsp baking powder
2 tsp bicarbonate of soda
255ml (10fl oz) buttermilk
3 large eggs
3½ tbsp blueberry or strawberry jam, plus extra for filling

For the frosting

190g (7oz) smooth peanut butter
455g (1lb) full-fat cream cheese, such as Philadelphia, cold
2 tsp vanilla extract
⅛ tsp salt
450g (1lb) icing sugar, sifted
2–3 tbsp whole milk

Three 20cm (8in) diameter loose-bottomed sandwich tins

In America a proper PB&J sandwich is made using grape jelly, which is a seedless grape jam. It's very hard to find in the UK, but you can use blueberry jam to mimic the purple fruitiness, and strawberry jam will also do at a pinch. A classic American combination in layer cake form!

1. To make the cake, preheat the oven to 170°C (325°F), Gas mark 3. Line the cake tins with non-stick baking parchment.
2. Using an electric mixer with the paddle attachment or a hand-held electric whisk, cream the butter, sugar, flour, baking powder and bicarbonate together until they form a sandy consistency.
3. In a large jug, mix together the buttermilk, eggs and the jam by hand. With the mixer on a medium speed, slowly pour half the liquid into the crumb mixture and mix together, scraping down the sides of the bowl as you go. When the lumps are gone, add the rest of the liquid and mix until combined.
4. Divide the batter evenly between the three prepared tins. Bake for 20–30 minutes until a deep golden brown and the sponge bounces back when lightly touched. Cool the sponges in the tins for about 10 minutes, and then turn out to cool completely on wire racks.
5. To make the frosting, using a freestanding electric mixer with the paddle attachment or a hand-held electric whisk, beat the peanut butter on a medium speed until light and fluffy. Add the cream cheese, vanilla extract and salt and beat on a low speed for a minute until everything is well mixed and smooth – do not overbeat or the cream cheese will split and become too runny.
6. Gradually add the icing sugar, on a low speed, until it is all incorporated. Add 2 tablespoons of the milk and beat until smooth and easy to spread. Add another tablespoon of milk if the mixture is too thick.
7. Spread a good layer of jam on top of the first and second layers of sponge. Spread 3–4 tablespoons of the frosting on top of the jam, then sandwich the layers together and put the third layer on top. Spread the rest of the frosting over the top and sides of the cake.

Chocolate Doberge Cake

**Makes one 20cm (8in)
cake, to slice as desired**

For the cake

3 large eggs, separated

270g (9½oz) plain flour,
sifted

1 tsp bicarbonate of soda

1 tsp salt

60g (2oz) very dark
chocolate (90–99%
cocoa solids, such
as Lindt Excellence)

140g (5oz) unsalted butter,
softened

320g (11oz) caster sugar

235ml (8fl oz) full-fat
buttermilk

1¼ tsp vanilla extract

1 tsp almond extract

For the custard

585ml (1 pint) evaporated
milk (unsweetened)

60g (2oz) dark chocolate
(minimum 70% cocoa
solids)

270g (9½oz) caster sugar

45g (1½oz) plain flour

4 large egg yolks, lightly
beaten

30g (1oz) unsalted butter

1¼ tsp vanilla extract

¼ tsp almond extract

The Doberge cake is from New Orleans and the locals pronounce it 'dough-bosh'. This chocolate version consists of layers of thin chocolate sponge filled with chocolate custard, frosted with chocolate buttercream and glazed with a ganache. This recipe definitely needs time, effort and experience, but will be well worth the effort in wowing your friends and family.

1. To make the cake, preheat the oven to 150°C (300°F), Gas mark 2. Line the tins with non-stick baking parchment.

2. Using a freestanding electric mixer with the whisk attachment or a hand-held electric whisk, beat the egg whites to stiff peak stage, so they curl when the beaters are lifted. Set aside.

3. In a bowl, sift together the flour, bicarbonate of soda and salt three times. Set aside.

4. Melt the chocolate in a microwave-safe bowl in the microwave or in a medium-sized heatproof bowl set over, but not touching, a pan of simmering water.

5. Using the electric mixer with the paddle attachment or a hand-held electric whisk, cream the butter and sugar together for around 5 minutes on a medium–high speed until light and fluffy.

6. Add the egg yolks on a lower speed and mix together well, being sure to scrape down the sides of the bowl as you go to make sure everything is well combined. Add the flour mix and buttermilk in thirds, alternating between the two. Don't overbeat – only mix after each addition until the flour and buttermilk disappear into the mixture.

7. Add the melted chocolate and beat on the lowest speed to thoroughly mix. Finally, fold the egg whites into the batter by hand, and then mix in the vanilla and almond extracts.

8. Divide the batter between the three prepared tins and bake for 35–40 minutes or until the sponges bounce back when lightly touched. Cool the sponges in the tins for about 10 minutes, and then turn out to cool completely on wire racks.

9. To make the custard, combine the evaporated milk and chocolate in a saucepan and cook over a medium heat until the chocolate melts.

10. In a bowl, combine the sugar and flour, stirring with a fork to mix. Slowly add about a third of the chocolate mixture, tablespoon by tablespoon, to the sugar and flour and stir to make a smooth paste. Scrape the paste back into the saucepan with the rest of the milk and chocolate and cook over a medium heat for about 3 minutes until it thickens.

11. Now, stir about 80ml (3fl oz) of the warm chocolate mix into the beaten egg yolks in order to warm them up – keep stirring so that the eggs don't scramble. Then add the warmed-up egg yolks to the saucepan with the rest of the mix and stir well so that they are mixed thoroughly and quickly.

12. Cook for a further 5 minutes or until the custard is thick, shiny and smooth. Take off the heat, add the butter, vanilla and almond extracts and stir well until thoroughly mixed. Scrape the custard onto a baking sheet, cover the surface with cling film to prevent a skin forming and refrigerate while you make the frosting.

13. Using a freestanding electric mixer with the paddle attachment or a hand-held electric whisk, beat the butter on a medium-high speed for 2 minutes to loosen it.

14. Melt the chocolate in a microwave-safe bowl in the microwave or in a medium-sized heatproof bowl set over, but not touching, a pan of simmering water.

15. Sift the icing sugar into a bowl with the cocoa powder then add it slowly to the butter, alternating with the vanilla and melted chocolate. Once incorporated, turn up the speed to high and beat for 3 minutes. If the mixture is too thick after about 3 more minutes of beating, then add a few tablespoons of hot water, one at a time, until a spreadable, light consistency is achieved. Set aside at room temperature until ready to use.

16. To make the ganache, place the chocolate in a bowl. Heat the cream and vanilla gently in a small saucepan until barely bubbling, then pour over the chocolate and leave to stand for 5 minutes before stirring until smooth. Leave this at room temperature for about 1 hour to cool to a spreading consistency.

17. To assemble the cake, cut each cake layer in half horizontally so that you end up with six thin layers. It's best to use a serrated knife and a sawing motion. Gently cut around the edge of the cake first, and then through the centre. Place one layer, top side down, on a plate or cake card, then put 10 tablespoons of custard on top and spread evenly over the layer. Cover with the other half of the same cake, bottom side up. Continue spreading custard between the layers and sandwiching them together, but don't put the custard on the top of the sixth layer – you should have used up all the custard by now. Cover the cake with cling film and put into the fridge for about 30 minutes.

▼

For the frosting
335g (12oz) unsalted butter, softened
40g (1½oz) dark chocolate (minimum 70% cocoa solids)
375g (13oz) icing sugar
120g (4oz) cocoa powder
2 tsp vanilla extract

For the ganache
200g (7oz) dark chocolate (minimum 70% cocoa solids), chopped
200ml (7fl oz) double cream
2 tsp vanilla extract

Three 20cm (8in) diameter loose-bottomed sandwich tins

18. Beat the cooled frosting well and spread over the top and sides of the cake. It's best if you then refrigerate the cake for a minimum of 1 hour.

19. Finally, spoon most of the ganache onto the top of the cake. Use a palette knife to smooth it over the top and down the sides of the cake, patching as necessary with the reserved ganache. The cake is best if then cooled for a few more hours or overnight, but be sure to remove it from the fridge at least 2 hours before serving.

Lady Baltimore Cake

**Makes one 20cm (8in)
cake, to slice as desired**

For the filling

75g (2½oz) raisins or
   sultanas (or a mix of both)
75g (2½oz) dried figs or
   dates, finely chopped
70g (2½oz) pecans,
   finely chopped
50ml (1¾fl oz) rum
   or brandy

For the cake

270g (9½oz) plain flour
2 tsp baking powder
½ tsp salt
1 tsp vanilla extract
235ml (8fl oz) whole milk
115g (4oz) unsalted butter,
   softened
320g (11oz) caster sugar
4 large egg whites

For the frosting

430g (15oz) caster sugar
4 large egg whites
120ml (4fl oz) golden syrup
½ tsp salt
½ tsp cream of tartar
2 tsp vanilla extract

*Three 20cm (8in) diameter
loose-bottomed sandwich
tins*

This Southern speciality will definitely make an impression at
any party – white, pillowy sponge layers, filled with dried fruits
and frosted with the lightest Southern boiled meringue frosting.
The unused egg yolks can be frozen individually in ice cube trays;
just add a pinch of sugar to each yolk and whisk for a second
or two before freezing.

1. To make the filling, mix the dried fruits and nuts in a bowl
with the alcohol and set aside for at least 1 hour, and preferably
24 hours, to soak the fruits and nuts really well.
2. To make the cake, preheat the oven to 170°C (325°F), Gas mark 3.
Line the three tins with non-stick baking parchment.
3. In a bowl, sift together the flour, baking powder and salt. In a large
jug, add the vanilla to the milk and set aside.
4. Using a freestanding electric mixer with the paddle attachment,
or a hand-held electric whisk, cream together the butter and sugar
at a high speed for at least 5 minutes until light and fluffy. Scrape
down the sides of the bowl and then add the milk and vanilla at a
lower speed mixing until just incorporated. If the mixture starts to
split, add a tablespoon of the dry ingredients and continue mixing.
With the mixer still running at low speed, add the dry ingredients in
one steady stream and stop beating when just incorporated. Take a
spatula and mix gently by hand, scraping down the sides of the bowl.
5. Beat the egg whites using a freestanding electric mixer with the
whisk attachment or a hand-held electric whisk until at firm peak
stage – be careful not to overbeat or they will become dry. Fold the
egg whites carefully into the cake mixture by hand, and when all
is mixed, divide between the three prepared tins.
6. Bake for about 25 minutes until the sponge is golden on top
and bounces back when lightly touched. Cool in the tins for
5 minutes, and then turn out onto wire racks to cool completely.
7. To make the frosting, bring some water to the boil in a small pan.
In a heatproof bowl set above, but not touching, the boiling water,
mix together the sugar, egg whites, syrup, salt and cream of tartar,
beating with a hand-held electric whisk for at least 12 minutes
until it holds stiff peaks. When you lift away the beaters, the peaks
formed should hold nicely. Remove the bowl from the heat, mix in
the vanilla and beat for 1–2 minutes more.

▼

8. To assemble the filling, take a third of the frosting and mix well with the fruit and nut mixture.

9. To assemble the cake, put one layer of sponge onto a plate or cake card. Spoon half the fruit and nut filling onto the sponge and spread evenly. Cover with a second layer of sponge and top with the other half of the fruit and nut filling, spreading it out evenly. Place the third sponge on top and then cover the sides and top of the cake with the remaining two-thirds of the frosting.

10. Use a palette knife to create swirls and peaks, making the most of the glossy smooth frosting for decorative effect.

Gingerbread Icebox Cake

Southern bakers had plenty of time on their hands and many older recipes do have many steps and processes to create that show-stopping star. This icebox cake involves making gingerbread wafers and arranging them into a tower held together with cinnamon whipped cream. We suppose you could buy the ginger biscuits, but making them is half the fun!

1. To make the wafers, in a large bowl, sift together the flour, ginger, cinnamon, cloves, bicarbonate of soda, baking powder and salt. Set aside.

2. Using a freestanding electric mixer with the paddle attachment or a hand-held electric whisk, cream the butter and sugar together for around 5 minutes on a medium-high speed until light and fluffy. Add the eggs, one at a time, on a lower speed, scraping down the sides of the bowl between additions. Continue mixing on a low speed and add the molasses. Add the dry ingredients in one go and continue to mix, scraping down the sides of the bowl, until a dough is formed.

3. Divide the dough into four equal amounts and shape each quarter into an oblong about 2.5cm (1in) thick. Wrap in cling film and refrigerate for at least 2 hours until the dough is firm enough to roll out.

4. Preheat the oven to 175°C (350°F), Gas mark 4. Line four baking sheets with non-stick baking parchment.

5. Once the dough is cold and firm, lightly flour a work surface and roll out the dough with a rolling pin to about 3mm (⅛in) thick. Cut out the wafers using a 6cm (2½in) round cutter. Place the wafers 2–3cm (1in) apart on the lined baking sheets. Use up as much of the dough as possible to make about seventy wafers. If the dough gets too warm, put it back into the fridge to cool down and get harder. If there is leftover dough, you can use it later, as this dough will last several days in the refrigerator or 2–3 months in the freezer.

6. Bake the wafers for 12–14 minutes until the edges are slightly darker and the tops of the wafers are firm to the touch. Cool on the sheets for about 10 minutes, then transfer to wire racks to cool completely while you make the filling.

▼

For the gingerbread wafer biscuits

670g (1lb 7oz) plain flour
1 tbsp ground ginger
1 tbsp ground cinnamon
1 tsp ground cloves
¾ tsp bicarbonate of soda
¼ tsp baking powder
½ tsp salt
170g (6oz) unsalted butter, softened
160g (5½oz) soft light brown sugar
2 large eggs
175g (6oz) pure cane molasses, such as Meridian

For the cream filling

585ml (1 pint) whipping cream
¾ tsp ground cinnamon
1 tsp vanilla extract
4 tbsp icing sugar

6cm (2½in) round cutter

7. In the bowl of a freestanding electric mixer with the whisk attachment or using a hand-held electric whisk, beat the cream, cinnamon, vanilla and icing sugar on high speed until soft peaks form.
8. To assemble the cake, spread 2 tablespoons of the whipped cream onto your cake plate to hold the first layer down, then place six wafers in a circle with the sides touching each other, and one more wafer in the centre. Put about 8 tablespoons of the cream on top and spread it evenly to cover most of the wafers, leaving the outside edge of the outer wafers uncovered. Repeat with seven more wafers, but this time offset the wafers so that they stack up in between the wafers below and not directly on top. Repeat until you have ten layers of wafers, covering the top with the last of the whipped cream. Refrigerate overnight, covering with an upturned cake tin if you like.

German Chocolate Cake

Makes one 20cm (8in) cake, to slice as desired

For the cake
120ml (4fl oz) boiling water
115g (4oz) 40-50% cooking chocolate (not very bitter)
270g (9½oz) plain flour
1 tsp bicarbonate of soda
1 tsp salt
60g (2oz) cocoa powder
225g (8oz) unsalted butter, softened
430g (15oz) caster sugar
4 large eggs, separated
1 tsp vanilla extract
235ml (8fl oz) buttermilk

For the frosting
190g (7oz) pecans, finely chopped
215g (7½oz) caster sugar
350ml (12fl oz) evaporated milk (unsweetened)
110g (4oz) unsalted butter
3 large egg yolks
1 tsp vanilla extract
200g (7oz) coconut flakes

Three 20cm (8in) diameter loose-bottomed sandwich tins

This cake is not from Germany, but is made in the US with 'German's Sweet Chocolate', named after Samuel German, who developed a baking short-cut: dark chocolate with all the sugar already added.

1. To make the cake, preheat the oven to 175°C (350°F), Gas mark 4. Line the three tins with non-stick baking parchment.
2. In a medium heatproof bowl, pour the boiling water over the chocolate. Stir until smooth and set aside.
3. In a separate bowl, sift together the flour, bicarbonate of soda and salt. Mix in the cocoa powder with a whisk or fork.
4. Using an electric mixer with the paddle attachment or a hand-held electric whisk, cream the butter and sugar together for around 5 minutes on a medium-high speed until light and fluffy. Add the egg yolks, one at a time, scraping down the sides of the bowl after each addition, until well incorporated. Reduce the mixer speed to low and add the cool chocolate mixture and the vanilla. Add the flour mixture, in thirds, alternating with the buttermilk and ending with the flour.
5. Using a freestanding electric mixer with the whisk attachment or a hand-held electric whisk, beat the egg whites to soft peak stage. By hand, gently fold the beaten whites into the batter in about three additions.
6. Divide the batter between the prepared tins, smoothing the tops with the back of a spoon, then bake for 30 minutes until the sponge bounces back when lightly touched. Cool in the tins for about 15 minutes and then turn out to cool completely on wire racks.
7. To make the frosting, first toast the pecans in a dry frying pan on a medium heat. Be careful, as this should only take about 30–60 seconds and they can burn quickly.
8. In a medium saucepan, combine the sugar, milk, butter, egg yolks and vanilla. Cook over a low heat, stirring constantly, for 15–20 minutes until thickened. Stir in the coconut and pecans. Transfer to a bowl and, stirring occasionally, allow to cool to room temperature before frosting the cake.
9. To assemble the cake, place one layer on a plate or cake card and spread with a third of the frosting. Repeat with the next layer, sandwiching them together, then spread the rest of the frosting over the top and sides of the cake.

Lemon Doberge Cake

Makes one 20cm (8in) cake, to slice as desired

For the lemon custard
270g (9½oz) caster sugar
3 tbsp cornflour
3 tbsp plain flour
Pinch of salt
350ml (12fl oz) cold water
3 large egg yolks, lightly beaten
30g (1oz) unsalted butter
Zest of 2 lemons
80ml (3fl oz) fresh lemon juice

For the cake
3 large egg whites
300g (10½oz) plain flour
2 tsp baking powder
¼ tsp salt
170g (6oz) unsalted butter, softened
140g (5oz) caster sugar
1 tsp vanilla extract
1 tsp lemon extract
3 large egg yolks, at room temperature
60ml (2fl oz) fresh lemon juice
120ml (4fl oz) whole milk

Like the chocolate Doberge, this cake made with lemon also hails from New Orleans, where it's common for bakeries to sell half a lemon cake and half a chocolate cake placed together, to form a single mix-and-match Doberge.

1. To make the lemon custard, combine the sugar, cornflour, plain flour and salt in a saucepan. Stir in the cold water and cook on a medium heat until the mixture thickens and bubbles, stirring frequently, then cook for a further 2 minutes.

2. Put the beaten egg yolks into a bowl and slowly pour in about a third of the hot flour and sugar mixture in order to warm up the egg yolks. Stir quickly so that the yolks do not cook. Pour the warmed-up yolks into the remaining flour and sugar mixture in the saucepan and bring to a gentle boil. Stir constantly and cook for 2–3 more minutes, then remove from the heat. Stir in the butter, lemon zest and fresh

For the lemon frosting
255g (9oz) full-fat
  cream cheese, such as
  Philadelphia, cold
560g (1lb 3oz) icing sugar,
  sifted
2 tsp finely chopped
  lemon zest
½ tsp vanilla extract
½ tsp lemon extract

*Three 20cm (8in) diameter
loose-bottomed sandwich
tins*

lemon juice and mix well. Scrape into a bowl, cover with cling film, pressing it directly onto the surface to prevent a skin forming, and cool to room temperature – do not stir further.

3. To make the cake, preheat the oven to 175°C (350°F), Gas mark 4. Line the three tins with non-stick baking parchment.

4. Using a freestanding electric mixer with the whisk attachment or a hand-held electric whisk, beat the egg whites to stiff peak stage. In a bowl, sift together the flour, baking powder and salt three times.

5. Using the electric mixer with the paddle attachment or a hand-held electric whisk, cream the butter and sugar together for 5 minutes on a medium-high speed until light and fluffy. Add the vanilla and lemon extracts and the egg yolks and mix until well incorporated.

6. In a jug, mix together the lemon juice and milk. Add to the creamed mixture with the dry ingredients, alternating in thirds, mixing after each addition. Only mix until each ingredient is just incorporated. Scrape down the sides of the bowl often. After the final addition, mix well for another minute until smooth and light. Fold in the egg whites by hand.

7. Divide the batter evenly between the three prepared tins and bake for 25–30 minutes or until the sponges are golden brown and bounce

▼

back when lightly touched. Cool the sponges in the tins for about 10 minutes, and then turn out to cool completely on wire racks.

8. To make the frosting, using a freestanding electric mixer with the paddle attachment or a hand-held electric whisk, beat the cream cheese and icing sugar together for 2–3 minutes until light and fluffy – do not overbeat or the cream cheese will split. Mix in the lemon zest and vanilla and lemon extracts.

9. To assemble the cake, cut each cake in half horizontally so that you end up with six thin layers. It's best to use a serrated knife and a sawing motion. Gently cut around the edge of the cake first and then through the centre.

10. Place one layer on a plate or cake card, then put 3–4 tablespoons of custard on top and spread evenly over the layer. Cover with the other half of the same cake. Continue spreading custard between the layers and sandwiching them together, but don't put custard on the sixth layer. Cover with cling film and put into the fridge for about 30 minutes.

11. Finally, spread the frosting over the top and sides of the cake. The cake is best if cooled for a few more hours or overnight, but remove the cake from the fridge at least 2 hours before serving.

Alabama Little Layer Cake

Makes one 20cm (8in) cake, to slice as desired

For the cake
280g (10oz) unsalted butter
670g (1lb 7oz) caster sugar
100g (3½oz) vegetable
    shortening (Trex)
6 large eggs
2½ tsp vanilla extract
845g (1¾lb) plain flour
1¼ tsp salt
2½ tsp bicarbonate
    of soda
6½ tsp baking powder
590ml (1 pint) whole milk

For the frosting
1kg (2lb 3oz) caster sugar
40g (1½oz) cocoa powder
115g (4oz) unsalted butter,
    cut into pieces
350ml (12fl oz) evaporated
    milk (unsweetened)
120ml (4fl oz) whole milk
2 tsp vanilla extract

Three 20cm (8in) diameter loose-bottomed sandwich tins and a sugar thermometer

This traditional recipe from south-eastern Alabama is from the days before electric whisks and icing sugar existed. Frostings used to be boiled, and carefully cooking this one correctly is crucial. This recipe needs a lot of time and is not for the novice baker – however, the result will wow everyone!

1. To make the cake, preheat the oven to 200°C (400°F), Gas mark 6. Grease the three tins and base line with non-stick baking parchment.
2. Using a freestanding electric mixer with the paddle attachment or a hand-held electric whisk, cream together the butter, sugar and shortening at a high speed for at least 4–5 minutes until light and fluffy. Lower the speed to medium and add the eggs, one at a time, scraping down the sides of the bowl after each addition. When all the eggs have been added, mix until everything is well incorporated. Stir in the vanilla.
3. In a large bowl, sift together the flour, salt, bicarbonate of soda and baking powder twice. You want everything to be light and airy. Add the sifted dry ingredients and the milk to the creamed ingredients in several additions, starting with the dry and alternating with the milk, then finishing with the dry. Beat for a further 2–3 minutes on a medium speed until all is smooth and mixed, scraping down the sides of the bowl as you go. Measure out about 230g (8oz) of batter into each prepared tin, smoothing down lightly with a spatula to get an even layer.
4. Bake for 8–10 minutes, or until the sponge is golden brown and bounces back when lightly touched. Take out of the oven and immediately turn out onto a wire rack. Repeat with the rest of the batter until you've got at least twelve layers. You can reuse the parchment, but be sure to clean the tins of any cooked-on batter.
5. While the first layers are in the oven, start to make the frosting. Put the sugar and cocoa in a large, deep saucepan and mix well. Turn the heat to medium–high, then add the butter, evaporated milk and whole milk and bring to a boil. Boil for about 4 minutes, stirring continuously. Be careful and keep watching the saucepan to make sure that the mixture does not boil over. Reduce the heat to low, add the vanilla and simmer, stirring occasionally, for another 7–10 minutes. Using a sugar thermometer, cook to the point just before soft ball stage, or about 110°C (230°F).

▼

6. While the second batch of layers is in the oven and the first batch is still warm, begin to assemble the cake. Put one layer on a plate or cake card, with the top side facing upwards. Put about 4 tablespoons of the warm frosting on top. This frosting will seem thin, but it thickens as it cools. Spread all over to cover the first layer. Stack on the second layer, again with the top side facing up, and put 4 more tablespoons of frosting on top of that. Continue until you have used all twelve sponges. Cover the top of the cake with the remaining frosting, allowing it to drizzle down the sides of the cake stack.

Orange Layer Cake

Makes one 20cm (8in) cake, to slice as desired

For the cake

340g (12oz) plain flour
320g (11oz) caster sugar
2 tsp baking powder
¼ tsp bicarbonate of soda
1 tsp salt
115g (4oz) unsalted butter, softened
Grated zest of 1 orange
60ml (2fl oz) freshly squeezed orange juice
175ml (6fl oz) whole milk
2 large eggs

For the filling

30g (1oz) unsalted butter
50g (1¾oz) caster sugar
2 large eggs, beaten
1 tbsp orange zest
1 tbsp fresh lemon juice
115ml (4fl oz) freshly squeezed orange juice
1 tsp orange liqueur

For the custard frosting

40g (1½oz) caster sugar
1 tbsp cornflour
115ml (4fl oz) evaporated milk (unsweetened)
3 large egg yolks
115ml (4fl oz) freshly squeezed orange juice
1 tsp orange zest

Three 20cm (8in) diameter loose-bottomed sandwich tins

Another traditional style recipe from the old South that calls for several processes, including boiling the frosting and filling. Cointreau, Triple Sec or Grand Marnier can be used for the filling.

1. Preheat the oven to 175°C (350°F), Gas mark 4. Line the three tins with non-stick baking parchment.
2. To make the cake, sift the dry ingredients into the bowl of a freestanding electric mixer or a bowl you can use a hand-held electric whisk in. Add the butter and, starting with the mixer on a low speed, beat until combined. Add the orange zest and orange juice. Beat for 2 minutes, scraping down the sides of the bowl as you go. Add the milk and eggs and beat for 2 minutes longer.
3. Divide the batter between the three prepared tins. Bake for 25–30 minutes until the sponges are golden and bounce back when lightly touched. Cool in the tins for about 10 minutes, then turn out onto wire racks to cool completely.
4. To make the filling, place all the ingredients in a heatproof bowl set over, but not touching, a pan of simmering water and cook, stirring frequently, for about 20 minutes until the mixture has thickened and coats the back of a spoon. Pour into a bowl, cover the surface with cling film, pressing it directly onto the surface to prevent a skin forming, and chill until needed.
5. To make the custard frosting, mix the sugar and cornflour together in a large heatproof bowl. Add the evaporated milk and whisk together in the bowl set over, but not touching, a pan of simmering water until smooth and slightly thickened. Remove from the heat.
6. Using a freestanding electric mixer with the whisk attachment or a hand-held electric whisk, beat the egg yolks until light and thickened. Add the orange juice and zest and continue beating until combined. Pour the egg yolk mixture into the warm milk mixture, then set the bowl back over the pan of simmering water and continue cooking until the mixture is thickened and coats the back of a spoon. Pour into a bowl, cover the surface with cling film to prevent a skin forming, then chill.
7. To assemble the cake, put one layer of sponge on a plate or cake card. Cover with half of the filling. Place a second layer of sponge on top and cover with the remaining filling. Place the third layer on top. Spoon the custard frosting over the top of the cake, using a palette knife to push the frosting to the edges so that it dribbles over the sides.

Red Velvet Crepe Cake

Makes one 22cm (9in) cake, to slice as desired

For the crepe batter

120ml (4fl oz) water

230g (8oz) unsalted butter, cold and cubed

340g (12oz) white chocolate, chopped

110g (4oz) dark chocolate (minimum 70% cocoa solids), chopped

470g (1lb 1oz) plain flour

150g (5½oz) soft light brown sugar

1 tsp salt

940ml (1½ pints) whole milk

230ml (8fl oz) buttermilk

12 large eggs

6 large egg yolks (reserve 3 of the whites for the buttercream)

2 tbsp red gel paste colouring mixed in 2 tbsp water

2 tbsp vanilla extract

▼

A lot of ingredients go into this recipe, but once you've mixed it all up, assembling the crepes and meringue buttercream is quite simple. Crepe cakes are all the rage, so we naturally wanted to show you how to make a Red Velvet version!

1. To make the crepes, heat the water in a saucepan until it is almost boiling, then whisk in the cold butter, one cube at a time. Add the white and dark chocolate, shake the saucepan to even out the chocolate at the bottom of the pan, then take off the heat and set aside.

2. Put the dry ingredients into the bowl of a freestanding electric mixer with the paddle attachment, or a bowl you can use a hand-held electric whisk in, and mix together with a fork. Add the milk and buttermilk and mix on a low speed. Add the eggs and extra yolks, one at a time, mixing until just incorporated.

3. Whisk the melted chocolate – it will seem runny. Pour into the rest of the ingredients and mix on slow until all is incorporated – don't overmix. The mixture will seem relatively runny and will be a light brown (not very nice) colour. Pour all this into a large bowl and mix in the red colouring and vanilla extract. The resulting colour should be a light red or dark pink. Put into the freezer to allow to cool down, thicken and relax for 10 minutes.

4. To make the meringue buttercream, using the electric mixer with the paddle attachment or a hand-held electric whisk, beat the butter, icing sugar and vanilla seeds (or extract) together, then add the cold cream cheese and beat for 2–3 minutes until fluffy. Don't overbeat or the cream cheese will split and become too runny. Put into a bowl and set aside.

5. In a small saucepan, combine the caster and brown sugars and water over a medium–high heat and cook until it reaches the soft ball stage as measured on a sugar thermometer, about 120°C/248°F.

6. While the sugars are cooking, put the reserved egg whites into the bowl of the electric mixer with the whisk attachment or a bowl you can use a hand-held electric whisk in. When the sugar reaches soft ball stage, turn the mixer on to high speed and *slowly* pour the hot syrup down the inside of the bowl so that you don't splash yourself. Beat until stiff peaks form.

▼

For the meringue buttercream

250g (9oz) unsalted butter, softened
125g (4½oz) icing sugar
Seeds scraped from 1 vanilla pod (or 1½ tsp vanilla extract)
340g (12oz) full-fat cream cheese, such as Philadelphia, cold
110g (4oz) caster sugar
110g (4oz) soft light brown sugar
60ml (2fl oz) water
235ml (8fl oz) whipping cream

Sugar thermometer and a 22cm (9in) non-stick frying pan

7. Add the cream cheese mixture to the meringue about 4 tablespoons at a time while the mixer is on medium speed. Once it is all incorporated, beat for about 2 minutes until fluffy. Whisk the whipping cream until it forms soft peaks and fold into the meringue buttercream mix. Set aside in the fridge.

8. To cook the crepes, take the batter out of the freezer. Grease the non-stick pan with a light cooking oil. With the pan on a medium-high heat, pour 60ml (2fl oz) of batter into the pan. Each crepe takes about 1 minute to cook. When you pour the batter into the greased pan, twirl the pan to get the batter to fill the entire base of the pan. When the edges seem 'dry', run a spatula around the edge, turn over and cook on the other side for a few moments. Make at least thirty-two crepes – you may have a few extra. The first one or two crepes can be discarded if they don't turn out perfectly.

9. To assemble the cake, put the first crepe on a plate and, using a palette knife, smooth 1 heaped tablespoon of the meringue buttercream over the crepe, stopping just before the edge. Place the second crepe on top of the smoothed-on buttercream and repeat until all the crepes have been used up. Remember, you don't want a very thick layer of buttercream between the crepes, as there will be about thirty-two layers. Smooth the final bit of buttercream on top of the cake to finish.

Appalachian Stack Cake

In the Appalachian Mountains, wedding cakes were traditionally a community affair. Where money was short, friends and family would each bring a layer of cake and the most popular brides and grooms would have layer upon layer stacked high and filled with an apple preserve known as apple butter. We've only gone with six layers and we're showing you how to make your own version of apple butter, as it's not easily bought in the UK. The layers are more akin to cookies in texture than sponge. Well worth the time and effort!

1. To make the cake, preheat the oven to 175°C (350°F), Gas mark 4. Grease the three tins with butter and base line with non-stick baking parchment. You will need to re-use the three cake tins to make the six layers – you can re-use the parchment from each tin.
2. Using a freestanding electric mixer with the paddle attachment or a hand-held electric whisk, cream the butter and sugar together on a high speed for at least 4–5 minutes until light and fluffy. Add the buttermilk, molasses, egg and vanilla and continue to mix well.
3. In a large bowl, sift together the flour, ginger, bicarbonate of soda, salt, cinnamon and nutmeg. On a low speed, add the flour mixture to the creamed mixture and mix until just incorporated – don't overbeat the dough.
4. On a lightly floured surface, form the dough into a log and cut into six equal portions. Place one portion in each prepared tin. As you are using three tins to make six layers, you will need to do this in stages. Use your fingers to lightly press the dough into the edges of the tins.
5. Bake for 10–12 minutes or until lightly browned. Note that these make cookie-dough-like layers, similar to gingerbread cookies, not sponge layers. Remove the cake layers from the tins and cool completely on wire racks.
6. To make the apple butter, in a large saucepan combine the dried fruit and all the dry ingredients, including the vanilla pod. Add the Calvados or apple brandy, if using, and the pressed apple juice. The fruits will expand as they soak in the liquid, so make sure your saucepan is big enough.

Makes one 20cm (8in) cake, to slice as desired

For the cake
110g (4oz) unsalted butter, softened
110g (4oz) caster sugar
120ml (4fl oz) buttermilk
80g (3oz) pure cane molasses, such as Meridian
1 large egg
1 tsp vanilla extract
470g (1lb 1oz) plain flour
1 tsp ground ginger
½ tsp bicarbonate of soda
½ tsp salt
½ tsp ground cinnamon
Pinch of ground nutmeg

For the apple butter filling
400g (14oz) dried apples, roughly chopped
150g (5½oz) dark brown sugar
1 tsp ground ginger
1 tsp ground cinnamon
½ tsp ground cloves
½ tsp ground nutmeg
1 vanilla pod, split open and seeds reserved
2 tbsp Calvados or apple brandy (optional)
1.4 litres (2 pints 6fl oz) cloudy, pressed apple juice (not clear, from concentrate)

Icing sugar, for sprinkling
   on top

*Three 20cm (8in) diameter
loose-bottomed sandwich
tins*

7. Bring the mixture to a low boil and simmer for an hour or two, stirring often. Keep on cooking until you've got a dark, stew-like pulp. The apples may have broken down by this point, but this is fine as you'll be blitzing it afterwards. Remove from the heat, take out the vanilla pod and let stand for 30 minutes.

8. Transfer to a food processor, add the reserved vanilla seeds and process with the metal blade attachment until the mixture is smooth and forms a thick paste. Use while still lukewarm.

9. To assemble the stack cake, place one cake layer on a serving plate or cake card and spread with one-fifth of the warm apple butter filling. Repeat the procedure with the remaining cake layers and fruit butter filling, stacking each on the previous layer. Do not spread the fruit butter filling on the top layer. Cover the cake securely with cling film and refrigerate for at least 24 hours before serving with icing sugar sprinkled over the top.

Pies

Basic American Flaky Pastry
Strawberry Chiffon Pie
Lemon Chiffon Pie
Shaker Lemon Pie
Deep-fried Apple Pies
Peanut Butter Chocolate
   Banana Bacon Pie
Blueberry Cream Cheese Pie
Sliced Sweet Potato Pie
Blackberry Sonker
Vinegar Pie
Earl Grey Tea Pie
Piña Colada Icebox Pie
New Orleans Prune Pie

Basic American Flaky Pastry

**Makes enough for a
23cm (9in) pie dish**

180g (6½oz) plain flour
60g (2oz) very cold
   unsalted butter
55g (2oz) vegetable
   shortening (Trex)
   or unsalted butter
3 tbsp very cold water

One 23cm (9in) pie dish

A real American pie pastry should be very short, and vegetable shortenings are commonly used to achieve this. Using a mix of shortening and butter balances taste and lightness, and keeping everything ice cold – including your fingers – is essential.

1. To make the pastry, place all the ingredients except the water in a food processor with the blade attachment and pulse until it looks like breadcrumbs.
2. Add the water, pulsing again to bring the pastry together. Gather up the dough and use your hands to lightly form it into a ball. This is a very short pastry and it can seem a bit crumbly when handled. Try to bring it together in a few, firm movements until it sticks together. It won't be smooth or glossy. Wrap the pastry in cling film and put it in the fridge for 1 hour.
3. Remove the pastry from the fridge 10 minutes before you want to use it. Roll out the pastry on a lightly floured surface until just a bit bigger than your pie dish, being careful to use short rolls to avoid stretching the pastry too much.
4. Carefully line the pie dish, letting the pastry hang over the edge of the pie dish. Set aside in the fridge to chill for 1 hour. Once the pastry has chilled, trim any excess pastry from the edge with a small knife, cutting in line with the edge of the pie dish.
5. Blind-bake or fill your pastry case as directed in the recipe.

Strawberry Chiffon Pie

**Makes a 23cm (9in) pie,
to slice as desired**

For the crust
200g (7oz) digestive
  biscuits or Graham
  Crackers (see page 247)
80g (3oz) unsalted butter,
  melted

For the chiffon filling
550g (1lb 3oz) strawberries
  – frozen for at least
  48 hours
2 tsp fresh lemon juice
5 leaves of gelatine,
  weighing about 12g (½oz)
115ml (4fl oz) whipping
  cream
80g (3oz) caster sugar
1 large egg white
¼ tsp cream of tartar

*One 23cm (9in) pie dish
or foil pie dish*

This needs forward planning, so make sure you read the recipe carefully before you start. Americans use Graham Crackers for the crust – we show you how to make them on page 247.

1. To make the crust, using a food processor or a ziplock bag and a rolling pin, crush the biscuits to a fine crumb. In a mixing bowl, mix the crumbs with the melted butter until the mixture resembles wet sand and can be squeezed together. Press this into the base and up the sides of the pie dish and put into the refrigerator to set.
2. Several hours before making the filling, put the strawberries in a colander over a bowl and thaw out fully. As they're thawing out, put some pressure on them with a small plate to get more juice out. You will need about 295ml (10fl oz) of strawberry juice.
3. Over a medium heat, boil the strawberry juice in a saucepan for 10–15 minutes until it is reduced to about 60–65ml (2fl oz). Purée the leftover strawberries in a food processor until a smooth liquid

is formed. Take out of the processor and put into a bowl. Stir the reduced strawberry juice and the lemon juice into the strawberry purée and chill in the fridge for about 1 hour until it is cold.

4. Soak the gelatine leaves in a small heatproof bowl with 3 tablespoons cold water and set aside for 10–15 minutes to soften.

5. Using a freestanding electric mixer with the whisk attachment or a hand-held electric whisk, beat the cream with half the sugar on high speed until soft peaks form. Transfer the cream to a bowl and place in the fridge to keep cool.

6. Using a freestanding electric mixer with the whisk attachment or a hand-held electric whisk, beat the egg white until it is foamy, adding the cream of tartar while mixing. Add the remaining sugar and continue whisking until it reaches stiff peak stage.

7. Put the bowl of water and gelatine in the microwave and heat for 10 seconds or so (or place over a pan of boiling water). Then stir until the gelatine dissolves and the mixture is smooth. Add to the cold strawberry mixture, whisking continuously and vigorously. Fold in the egg white by hand, followed by the cold whipped cream, folding gently so as not to lose volume. Pour the filling into the cooled pie crust and allow to set in the fridge for about an hour.

Lemon Chiffon Pie

**Makes a 23cm (9in) pie,
to slice as desired**

1 x quantity Basic American
   Flaky Pastry (see page 92)
   or 500g (1lb 2oz) block
   shortcrust pastry or
   375g (13oz) ready-rolled
   shortcrust pastry

For the filling
3 leaves of gelatine,
   weighing 7g (⅓oz)
215g (7½oz) caster sugar
115ml (4fl oz) fresh lemon
   juice
60ml (2fl oz) water
½ tsp salt
4 large eggs, separated
Grated zest of 2 lemons

*One 23cm (9in) pie dish
or foil pie dish*

Chiffon pies have a light filling, usually cooked and firmed up with gelatine, then aerated by folding in beaten egg whites. As the egg whites are uncooked, please make sure you use free-range British Lion-stamped eggs. Chiffon pies come in all flavours, even savoury, but tangy lemon is one of our favourites.

1. Preheat the oven to 175°C (350°F), Gas mark 4.
2. To make the pastry, follow the Basic American Flaky Pastry recipe on page 92. If using shop-bought pastry, roll it out on a lightly floured surface until it is about 5mm (¼in) thick, line your pie dish and chill in the fridge for 1 hour.
3. Line the chilled pie crust loosely with baking parchment and fill with ceramic baking beans (or uncooked dried kidney beans). Blind-bake the pie crust for about 10 minutes. Remove the paper and beans and cook again for 20–25 minutes until nice and golden. Allow the pie crust to cool completely before filling.
4. To make the filling, soak the gelatine leaves in a small bowl of cold water and set aside for 10–15 minutes to soften.
5. Mix half the sugar with the lemon juice, water, salt and egg yolks in a heatproof bowl set over, but not touching, gently boiling water. Whisk over the boiling water until the mixture is thick enough to coat the back of a spoon.
6. Drain the gelatine leaves and squeeze out any excess water. Remove the bowl of egg yolks and sugar from the hot water and stir in the softened gelatine and lemon zest, stirring until the gelatine is completely dissolved. Cover with cling film and put into the fridge to cool for 15–20 minutes.
7. Meanwhile, using a hand-held electric whisk or a freestanding electric mixer with the whisk attachment, beat the egg whites, adding the remaining caster sugar in a steady stream and whisking until the egg whites reach stiff peak stage.
8. Take the lemon mixture out of the fridge and beat until fluffy. Fold into the egg whites carefully by hand. Pour into the baked pie crust and chill in the refrigerator for 3–4 hours until firm.

Shaker Lemon Pie

**Makes a 23cm (9in) pie,
to slice as desired**

2 x quantity Basic American
  Flaky Pastry (see page
  92) or
  2 x 500g (1lb 2oz) block
  shortcrust pastry or
  2 x 375g (13oz) ready-
  rolled shortcrust pastry

For the filling

2 unwaxed lemons
430g (15oz) caster sugar
4 large eggs, beaten well
2 tbsp plain flour
¼ tsp salt

Egg, for egg wash
Caster sugar, for sprinkling

*One 23cm (9in) pie dish
or foil pie dish*

The Shakers, from whom this pie originates, made sure to waste nothing. We have all admired their simple handicrafts and furniture styles, and this pie using whole lemons, rinds included, is a tangy and classic example of their elegant baking style.

1. To make the pastry, follow the Basic American Flaky Pastry recipe on page 92, up to the end of step 2. If using shop-bought pastry, keep chilled in the fridge.
2. To make the filling, trim the stem end and tip off each lemon. Slice the lemons as thinly as possible into paper-thin crossways circles, including the rind and pith. Try to save the juice as you are slicing. Now chop the lemon slices in half and place in a bowl. Add the sugar to the lemons and stir well. Cover and set aside at room temperature for at least 3 hours, stirring occasionally.
3. Preheat the oven to 235°C (450°F), Gas mark 8.
4. Take the pastry out of the fridge 10 minutes before you're going to use it to allow it to soften slightly. Roll out the pastry on a lightly floured surface into two flat circles, both of which should be around 30cm (12in) in diameter (enough to line the 23cm (9in) dish with around 3–5cm (1½in) extra around the edge).
5. Line the base of the pie dish with one of the pastry circles. Put it back into the fridge for about 10 minutes to relax, along with the other pastry circle, which will form the top of the pie.
6. Add the eggs, flour and salt to the bowl of lemons and sugar. Make sure all the ingredients are mixed evenly and pour into the lined pie dish.
7. Wet the edges of the pastry base with a little egg wash and cover with the reserved pastry circle to form the top, trimming away the excess pastry. Crimp the edges using your fingers or a fork. Cut some steam vents neatly into the top of the pie and decorate using any scraps of pastry rolled out and shaped like lemons. Brush with egg wash and sprinkle lightly with caster sugar.
8. Bake for 15 minutes, then reduce the heat to 190°C (375°F), Gas mark 5 and bake for 30–35 minutes until the filling is bubbling out of the vents and looks thick and the pastry is nicely browned. Let the pie cool to room temperature so that the filling has time to thicken, otherwise it will be very runny and scalding hot when sliced. You can cool the pie in the fridge to get a perfect slice.

Deep-fried Apple Pies

Makes about 15 pies

For the pastry
340g (12oz) plain flour
2½ tsp baking powder
¾ tsp bicarbonate of soda
¼ tsp salt
110g (4oz) very cold
   unsalted butter
155ml (5½fl oz) buttermilk

For the filling
350g (12oz) peeled, cored
   and finely sliced tart
   apples (such as Granny
   Smith – you can also
   mix in some Pink Lady
   if desired)
115ml (4fl oz) water
1 tsp fresh lemon juice
55g (2oz) caster sugar
½ tsp ground cinnamon
½ tsp ground nutmeg
2 x 1cm (½in) cube of
   butter per pie

About 1 litre (1¾ pints)
   vegetable oil, for frying
Icing sugar for dusting

As American as apple pie and as Southern as deep-frying, these little pies eaten warm with vanilla ice cream can't be beaten. Make sure that your frying oil is hot enough so that they turn out crispy and brown without being too oily.

1. To make the pastry, put the flour, baking powder, bicarbonate of soda, salt and butter into a food processor with the blade attachment, pulse to mix, then add the buttermilk and pulse again to bring the pastry together. Remove and roll into a ball, cover with cling film and place in the fridge to chill while you make the filling.
2. To make the filling, put the sliced apples into a saucepan and add the water and lemon juice. Cover the pan and cook over a low heat for 15 minutes – the apples should be tender, but not falling apart. Remove the apples from the heat and drain off the water. Carefully sprinkle in the sugar, cinnamon and nutmeg and make sure the apples are coated evenly.
3. Roll out the pastry on a lightly floured surface to 3–3.5mm (⅛in) thick, then cut out fifteen rounds 9cm (3½in) in diameter. Divide the apple mixture between the pastry rounds. Dot two butter cubes into the mixture. Moisten half of the edge of each round with water, then fold the dry half over the filling onto the moistened edge and crimp firmly with the prongs of a fork to seal in tightly. (You can also crimp with your fingers and thumbs if you are confident.)
4. In a deep saucepan or deep-fat fryer, heat the vegetable oil to 190°C (375°F). Test with a thermometer or drop in a crouton-sized piece of white bread – if it turns golden immediately then the oil is hot enough. Deep-fry the pies in batches of 3 or 4. Carefully place them in the hot oil using a slotted spoon and deep-fry for about 3 minutes – or until the pies are golden brown. They should rise to the surface, so turn them over to get both sides to cook evenly. Make sure you don't pierce the pastry otherwise the hot filling will come out and could splatter. Remove the pies from the pan using a slotted spoon, drain thoroughly and put onto kitchen paper to soak up any excess oil. Sprinkle with icing sugar and serve warm.

Peanut Butter Chocolate Banana Bacon Pie

Makes a 23cm (9in) pie, to slice as desired

For the peanut pie crust

1 x quantity Basic American Flaky Pastry (see page 92) or 500g (1lb 2oz) block shortcrust pastry or 375g (13oz) ready-rolled shortcrust pastry

30g (1oz) unsalted peanuts, blitzed in a food processor until fine (optional)

For the filling

3 ripe bananas

6 slices of bacon

50g (1¾oz) dark chocolate (minimum 70% cocoa solids)

125g (4½oz) peanut butter (smooth or crunchy)

400ml (14fl oz) whole milk

¼ tsp vanilla extract

4 large egg yolks

160g (5½oz) caster sugar

30g (1oz) plain flour

30g (1oz) cornflour

One 23cm (9in) pie dish or foil pie dish

An unabashed recipe with a lot going on to make it delicious. Of course you can omit the bacon if you don't eat it, and it'll still be wonderful.

1. To make the pastry, follow the Basic American Flaky Pastry recipe on page 92, but add the unsalted peanuts to the pastry ingredients if using. If you're using shop-bought pastry you can leave these out. If using shop-bought pastry, roll it out on a lightly floured surface until it is about 5mm (¼in) thick, line your pie dish, and chill in the fridge for 1 hour.

2. Preheat the oven to 170°C (325°F), Gas mark 3. Line the chilled pie crust loosely with baking parchment and fill with ceramic baking beans (or uncooked dried kidney beans). Blind-bake the pie crust for about 15 minutes or until the crust is light brown. Allow the pie to cool completely and trim the edges before filling.

3. Cut two of the bananas lengthways in half and then across into quarters and line them up on the base of the pie crust.

4. Put the bacon under a hot grill and cook until brown and crispy. Chop finely, setting aside one of the chopped slices in the fridge for a decoration.

5. In a medium-sized heatproof bowl set over, but not touching, gently boiling water, melt the chocolate and peanut butter together until well blended and smooth. Mix in the bacon, then pour over the bananas and set aside.

6. Now make the custard. Put 350ml (12fl oz) of the milk and the vanilla into a saucepan and bring to the boil over medium heat. Once it starts boiling, remove from the heat and cool very slightly.

7. Put the egg yolks, caster sugar, flour, cornflour and the rest of the milk into a separate bowl and mix vigorously with a fork or whisk, trying to get all the lumps out to make a smooth paste. Pour a little of the hot milk into the yolk mixture to warm it up, whisking briskly, then pour this into the rest of the milk mixture and stir well. Put back on the heat and bring to the boil, whisking continuously. Cook for 5-10 minutes until thick. Pour into a bowl, cover with cling film and leave to cool completely.

8. Once the custard is cool, spread smoothly over the pie and put into the fridge for about 3 hours. When ready to serve, sprinkle the reserved bacon and chopped, remaining banana over the top.

Blueberry Cream Cheese Pie

Serves 8–10

For the cream cheese pie crust

85g (3oz) unsalted butter

140g (5oz) plain flour

Pinch of salt

⅛ tsp baking powder

65g (2oz) full-fat cream cheese, such as Philadelphia, cold

1 tbsp very cold water

1 tsp white wine or cider vinegar

70g (2½oz) chopped pecans

For the blueberry filling

2 tbsp cornflour

115ml (4fl oz) water

Pinch of salt

215g (7½oz) caster sugar

1 tbsp golden syrup

280g (10oz) fresh blueberries

½ tsp fresh lemon juice

170g (6oz) full-fat cream cheese, such as Philadelphia

125g (4½oz) icing sugar

235ml (8fl oz) whipping cream

One 23cm (9in) pie dish or foil pie dish

This pie has a different style of pastry crust that is ever so slightly tangy and perfectly light and flaky, complementing the cream cheese filling and sweet blueberry topping.

1. To make the pie crust, cut the butter into small cubes and put them straight into the freezer for 30 minutes.

2. Mix the flour, salt and baking powder in a food processor with the blade attachment. Add the cream cheese and blitz for about 15–20 seconds until it resembles coarse sand. Add the frozen butter and pulse until none of the pieces of butter is bigger than a pea. Add the cold water and vinegar and continue pulsing until there are no large pieces of butter.

3. Gather the dough together with your hands and roll out on a floured surface until just a bit bigger than your pie dish, then carefully line the dish, leaving a 1cm (½in) lip over the edge. Prick the bottom of the pastry with a fork and push the chopped pecans into the surface. Place in the fridge for 1 hour.

4. To make the blueberry filling, whisk together the cornflour and water in a medium saucepan. Add the salt, 160g (5½oz) of the caster sugar, the syrup and all the blueberries. On a medium heat, bring to the boil and cook for 6 minutes or until the sauce has thickened. Remove from the heat and add the lemon juice. Stir well and allow to cool to room temperature. The filling will continue to thicken as it cools.

5. Preheat the oven to 170°C (325°F), Gas mark 3. Line the pie crust loosely with some baking parchment and fill with ceramic baking beans (or uncooked dried kidney beans). Blind-bake the pie crust for 8 minutes. Remove the beans and parchment and cook for a further 15–20 minutes until the crust is cooked and golden brown. Allow to cool completely and trim the edges.

6. Using a freestanding electric mixer with the paddle attachment or a hand-held electric whisk, beat the cream cheese with the icing sugar until fluffy – don't overbeat. With an electric whisk, in a separate bowl, whip the cream with the remaining caster sugar until soft peaks form. Fold the whipped cream into the cream cheese mixture by hand and spoon into the pie crust, evening out the filling and making it flat. Top with the cooked blueberries and refrigerate until chilled and fully set.

Sliced Sweet Potato Pie

Makes a 23cm (9in) pie,
to slice as desired

2 x quantity Basic
  American Flaky Pastry
  (see page 92) or
2 x 500g (1lb 2oz) block
  shortcrust pastry or
2 x 375g (13oz) ready-
  rolled shortcrust pastry

For the filling
4 medium sweet potatoes
  (about 1.35kg/3lb)
270g (9½oz) caster sugar
2 level tbsp plain flour
1 tsp ground allspice
½ tsp ground ginger
½ tsp ground nutmeg
¼ tsp ground cloves
80g (3oz) golden syrup
2 tbsp whipping cream
30g (1oz) very cold unsalted
  butter, chopped

Egg, for egg wash

One 23cm (9in) pie dish
or foil pie dish

This pie looks great when sliced, so be sure to cool it completely
to allow the filling to thicken. If the filling does run out when slicing,
spoon it on top of your serving to retain the flavour.

1. To make the pastry, follow the Basic American Flaky Pastry recipe
on page 92, up to the end of step 2.
2. Wash the sweet potatoes, keeping the skins on, and place them
whole into a large pot and cover with water. Bring to a boil over a
high heat and then reduce the heat to low to keep it gently boiling.
Cook the sweet potatoes for 20–30 minutes, until they are soft
enough to be sliced, but still maintain their shape.
3. Mix the dry ingredients for the filling in a bowl. Put the golden
syrup and cream into a jug.
4. Drain the sweet potatoes and cool so they are not too hot
to handle. Peel and slice lengthways into 5mm (¼in) strips.
5. Preheat the oven to 175°C (350°F), Gas mark 4.
6. Take the pastry out of the fridge 10 minutes before using. Roll out
the pastry on a lightly floured surface into two flat circles, both of
which should be around 30cm (12in) in diameter. Line the base of
the pie dish with one of the pastry circles. Put it back into the fridge
for about 10 minutes to relax, along with the other pastry circle,
which will form the top of the pie.
8. Place one layer of sweet potato strips in the pie crust. Sprinkle
with a third of the spice and flour mixture. Add another layer of
sweet potato strips and another third of the spice and flour
mixture. Finish with a final layer of the sweet potato strips. Add
a few remaining slices of the sweet potato strips to the centre
of the filling, so that it does not sink while cooking. Sprinkle with
the remaining third of the spice and flour mixture. Pour the
syrup and cream mixture carefully and evenly over the filling.
Place the chopped cold butter evenly on top of the filling.
9. Wet the edges of the pastry base with a little egg wash and
cover with the reserved pastry circle to form the top, trimming
away the excess pastry. Crimp the edges using your fingers or a fork.
Cut steam vents neatly into the top of the pie and brush the top
with egg wash.
10. Bake the pie for 50–55 minutes until the crust is brown and
the filling is bubbling. Cool to room temperature to allow the filling
to thicken before serving.

Blackberry Sonker

Serves 8-10

For the filling
750g (1lb 10oz) blackberries
215g (7½oz) caster sugar
30g (1oz) cornflour
2 tbsp plain flour
1 tsp ground cinnamon

For the biscuit topping
135g (5oz) plain flour
1 tsp baking powder
½ tsp bicarbonate of soda
¼ tsp salt
45g (1½oz) cold unsalted
    butter, cut into cubes
175ml (6fl oz) buttermilk
45g (1½oz) unsalted butter,
    melted

For the dip
470ml (16½fl oz) whole milk
110g (4oz) caster sugar
1 tbsp cornflour
1 tsp vanilla extract

*One 23cm (9in) deep
pie dish or 25cm (10in) cast-
iron skillet or ovenproof pan*

A sonker is a type of fruit cobbler from North Carolina, usually served with 'dip' – which is basically a thin custard. Instead of a cobbler topping, the sonker has larger lumps of biscuit to soak up the warm fruity filling.

1. Preheat the oven to 220°C (425°F), Gas mark 7. Butter the pie dish or skillet.
2. To make the filling, combine the blackberries, sugar, cornflour, flour and cinnamon in a bowl, stir through until everything is well mixed, then set aside for 15–30 minutes.
3. To make the biscuit topping, mix the flour, baking powder, bicarbonate of soda and salt in a bowl. With very cold, dry fingers, rub in the butter cubes until the mixture is crumbly and there are no butter pieces bigger than the size of a pea. Heap up the flour and butter mix and create a well, then pour in the buttermilk and, using a wooden spoon, mix the ingredients until just incorporated. Set aside.
4. To make the dip, heat the milk over a medium heat and bring to a gentle boil. Whisk the sugar and cornflour in another bowl, making sure all is well mixed, then add the boiling milk, along with the vanilla, whisking vigorously until everything is completely mixed and smooth.
5. Pour back into the saucepan, reduce the heat so the mix is gently simmering and cook for about 15–20 minutes, stirring frequently, until it's reduced by about half and thickened. Remove from the heat and pour into a jug, covering the top directly with cling film to prevent a skin forming. Set aside.
6. To assemble the sonker, put the blackberry mixture into the pie dish or skillet and place on a large baking sheet to catch any drips. Using a spoon, plop the biscuit batter onto the blackberries. Each 'mound' should be about 3 tablespoons. It doesn't have to be exact, but the surface should be covered with similar-sized 'biscuit' shapes.
7. Pour the melted butter over the biscuit topping and bake in the oven for 15 minutes, then reduce the heat to 175°C (350°F), Gas mark 4 and bake for an additional 20–25 minutes, until the biscuits are firm and golden brown. Cool for about 30 minutes. Pour the dip onto each portion and serve.

Vinegar Pie

**Makes a 23cm (9in) pie,
to slice as desired**

1 x quantity Basic
  American Flaky Pastry
  (see page 92) or
  500g (1lb 2oz) block
  shortcrust pastry or
  375g (13oz) ready-rolled
  shortcrust pastry

For the filling
320g (11oz) caster sugar
1 tbsp plain flour
¼ tsp salt
3 large eggs, beaten
55g (2oz) unsalted butter,
  melted
45ml (1½fl oz) evaporated
  milk (unsweetened)
40ml (1½fl oz) white cider
  vinegar (or white wine
  or white malt vinegar)

*One 23cm (9in) pie dish
or foil pie dish*

An unusual but favourite recipe that uses vinegar as the star
ingredient, giving this pie a sweet and slightly tangy taste,
reminiscent of the lemon custard in a lemon meringue pie –
this recipe will be a pleasant surprise. We suggest using white
cider vinegar, as it gives the best finished taste; however, any
white vinegar will be fine.

1. Preheat the oven to 175°C (350°F), Gas mark 4.
2. To make the pastry, follow the Basic American Flaky Pastry recipe
on page 92. If using shop-bought pastry, roll it out on a lightly
floured surface until it is about 5mm (¼in) thick and line your pie
dish. Crimp the edges to suit your decorative style and chill in the
fridge for 1 hour.
3. Using a fork, combine the sugar, flour and salt in a bowl until
well mixed. Add the eggs, melted butter and evaporated milk.
With a whisk, beat to mix well, then add the vinegar and continue
whisking until the liquid is thick and smooth.
4. Pour the filling into the pie crust and bake for 10 minutes,
then reduce the oven temperature to 165°C (325°F), Gas mark
3 and bake for another 35–45 minutes. The pie is ready when the
centre is relatively firm and wiggles just slightly if the dish is moved.
Remove the pie and allow to cool completely – it will set further
as it cools down and should have a nice brown crust on the surface.

Earl Grey Tea Pie

Makes a 23cm (9in) pie, to slice as desired

1 x quantity Basic American Flaky Pastry (see page 92) or 500g (1lb 2oz) block shortcrust pastry or 375g (13oz) ready-rolled shortcrust pastry

For the filling
225g (8oz) unsalted butter, softened
430g (15oz) caster sugar
8 large egg yolks
175ml (6fl oz) strong Earl Grey tea, lukewarm
1 tbsp fresh lemon juice
1 tsp grated mandarin zest (or clementine, tangerine or orange zest)
2 tbsp plain flour
1½ tsp yellow cornmeal (polenta)
½ tsp salt

One 23cm (9in) pie dish or foil pie dish

Tea in the South is drunk often, but almost always iced and sweet. We have used Earl Grey tea to give added flavour to this recipe, but any black tea of your choice can be used. If you are not using Earl Grey, which is flavoured with bergamot, you can omit the grated fruit zest.

1. Preheat the oven to 175°C (350°F), Gas mark 4.
2. To make the pastry, follow the Basic American Flaky Pastry recipe on page 92. If using shop-bought pastry, roll it out on a lightly floured surface until it is about 5mm (¼in) thick and line your pie dish. Crimp the edges to suit your decorative style and chill in the fridge for 1 hour.
3. Using a freestanding electric mixer with the paddle attachment or a hand-held electric whisk, cream the butter and sugar together for around 5 minutes on a medium-high speed until light and fluffy.
4. Add the egg yolks, one at a time, on a lower speed, scraping down the sides of the bowl after each addition. Carefully add the tea, lemon juice and mandarin zest to the mixture and mix in well. On a low speed, add the flour, cornmeal and salt – don't overbeat at this stage.
5. Pour the filling into the pie crust and bake for about 45 minutes. The pie should be quite firm, but still have a little wobble when you move the dish. Cool completely before serving – it will set as it cools down.

Piña Colada Icebox Pie

**Makes a 23cm (9in) pie,
to slice as desired**

For the crust
14 shortbread finger
   biscuits
10 pecan halves
65g (2oz) unsalted butter,
   melted

For the filling
70g (2½oz) caster sugar
2 tbsp cornflour
225g (8oz) chopped
   pineapple (tinned is fine)
2 tbsp rum (optional)
225g (8oz) full-fat
   cream cheese, such as
   Philadelphia, softened
350ml (12fl oz) coconut
   cream
2 large eggs
235ml (8fl oz) whipping
   cream

Coconut flakes or
   shavings, to decorate
Pineapple wedges,
   to garnish

*One 23cm (9in) pie dish
or foil pie dish*

This fruity cocktail-inspired dessert is best served cold, and has a crust that will take kindly to being refrigerated. Make sure the baked filling is cold to the touch before you spread on the whipped cream. Use your creativity with the coconut and pineapple decorations to make the pie suit your decorating style.

1. To make the crust, preheat the oven to 175°C (350°F), Gas mark 4.
2. Blitz together the shortbread and pecan halves in a food processor and mix in the melted butter to form a wet, sandy texture. Press the mixture into the base and up the sides of the pie dish. Bake for 10–12 minutes until the crust is lightly brown. Cool completely – this will take at least 30 minutes.
3. To make the filling, mix the sugar and cornflour together in a small saucepan, stir in the chopped pineapple, its juice and the rum, if using, and heat until it starts to boil. Keep stirring and cook for 1 minute until the mixture thickens. Remove from the heat and cool for about 20 minutes.
4. Preheat the oven again to 175°C (350°F), Gas mark 4.
5. Using a freestanding electric mixer with the paddle attachment or a hand-held electric whisk, beat the cream cheese for a few minutes until smooth, but don't overbeat or it will split. Add 235ml (8fl oz) of the coconut cream on a low speed and mix until well blended. Put the rest of the coconut cream into the fridge. Add the eggs, one at a time, scraping down the sides of the bowl well after each addition, mixing only until just incorporated.
6. Pour the cooled pineapple mixture into the pie base, and then spoon the cream cheese mixture on top of it.
7. Bake for 30–35 minutes until it is set. Cool completely for at least 1 hour at room temperature, then chill for 4 hours.
8. Using a freestanding electric mixer with the whisk attachment or a hand-held electric whisk, whip the cream until it starts to thicken. Add the rest of the coconut cream and continue beating until the soft peak stage. Spread this over the pie and decorate with the coconut shavings and extra pineapple.

New Orleans Prune Pie

Makes a 23cm (9in) pie, to slice as desired

1½ x quantity Basic American Flaky Pastry (see page 92) or 750g (1lb 10oz) block shortcrust pastry or 600g (1lb 5oz) ready-rolled shortcrust pastry

For the filling
450g (1lb) large pitted prunes
Juice of ½ lemon
15g (½oz) unsalted butter
215g (7½oz) caster sugar
4 tbsp Kentucky bourbon or whiskey
65g (2oz) pecans, chopped

Egg, for egg wash
Caster sugar, for sprinkling

One 23cm (9in) pie dish or foil pie dish

The soft prunes in this recipe break down while baking and form a very tasty filling that bubbles through the gaps in the crust. Making a lattice topping can take some practice, but it will always impress when the pie is served.

1. To make the pastry, follow the Basic American Flaky Pastry recipe on page 92 up to the end of step 2. If using shop-bought pastry, keep it in the fridge.
2. Take the chilled pastry out of the fridge 10 minutes before you're going to roll it out to allow it to soften slightly. Roll out half the pastry into a flat circle, about 30cm (12in) in diameter (enough to line the 23cm (9in) dish with about 3-5cm (1½in) extra around the edge).
3. Line the base of the pie dish with the pastry circle. Put this back into the fridge to relax while you make the filling, along with the remaining pastry, which will form the lattice top of the pie.
4. Preheat the oven to 175°C (350°F), Gas mark 4.
5. Mix the prunes, lemon juice, butter and sugar in a saucepan over a low heat. Cook until the mixture becomes thicker and more syrup-like. Remove from the heat and when it cools, stir in the bourbon or whiskey. Mix in the pecans and make sure all is thoroughly combined and mixed through. Pour into the lined pie dish.
6. On a lightly floured surface, roll the extra piece of pastry into a square about 5mm (¼in) thick, then cut into 1.5-2cm (⅔-¾in) strips, making sure they are all longer than the diameter of the tin.
7. Egg wash the edge of the pastry in the pie dish and start to weave the lattice topping. Lay about six strips across the pie, leaving a little gap between them, then run the other strips one by one across the top of the pie, weaving them up and down between the existing strips and leaving the edges hanging over the tin. Once the strips are in place, press the pastry down around the edges and cut off any excess, creating a neat finish. Brush the top of the lattice with egg wash and then sprinkle with sugar.
8. Bake for 45-55 minutes until the crust is brown and the filling is set. Let the pie cool thoroughly before serving.

Cookies & Candies

Ambrosia Cookies
Soft Molasses Cookies
Peanut Butter and Marshmallow
   Cookies
Black Pepper Cookies
Black and White Cookies
Vanilla-filled Chocolate
   Cookies
Cornmeal Cookies
Pumpkin and White Chocolate
   Cookies
Lemon Drops
Birthday Cake Cookies
Turtle Cookies
Pumpkin Caramels
Creamy Pecan Pralines
Divinity

Ambrosia Cookies

Makes 30 cookies

135g (5oz) plain flour
¼ tsp baking powder
½ tsp bicarbonate of soda
¼ tsp salt
115g (4oz) unsalted butter,
  softened
110g (4oz) caster sugar
150g (5½oz) soft light
  brown sugar
1 large egg
1 tsp vanilla extract
70g (2½oz) oatmeal (not
  rolled oats)
80g (3oz) raisins
80g (3oz) chopped dates
60g (3oz) chopped pecans
40g (1½oz) desiccated
  coconut

These cookies are probably named after an American variant of fruit salad, called Ambrosia salad, which contains fruits, coconut, pecans and cream. This cookie version should be soft and chewy, so don't let them bake too long in the oven. The dried fruits seem to melt into the dough, making them even more irresistible.

1. Preheat the oven to 190°C (375°F), Gas mark 5. Line four large baking sheets with non-stick baking parchment.
2. In a bowl, sift together the flour, baking powder, bicarbonate of soda and salt. Set aside.
3. Using a freestanding electric mixer with the paddle attachment or a hand-held electric whisk, cream the butter and sugars together for around 5 minutes on a medium-high speed until light and fluffy.
4. Add the egg and vanilla extract to the creamed butter, mixing well, then incorporate the sifted ingredients into the bowl. Mix in the oatmeal, dried fruits, nuts and coconut.
5. Using a tablespoon, shape the dough into balls (weighing about 30g (1oz) each). Place these 5cm (2in) apart on the prepared baking sheets.
6. Bake for 8–10 minutes until the cookie edges begin to brown slightly, then cool for 5 minutes before removing to a wire rack to cool completely.

Soft Molasses Cookies

Makes about 20 cookies

110g (4oz) unsalted butter,
softened
1½ tsp ground ginger
½ tsp ground cinnamon
¼ tsp ground nutmeg
¼ tsp ground mace
¼ tsp ground cloves
1 tsp salt
100g (3½oz) dark
muscovado sugar
115g (4oz) pure cane
molasses, such as Meridian
1 large egg
270g (9½oz) plain flour
1 tsp bicarbonate of soda
55ml (2fl oz) sour milk
(squeeze ½ lemon into
50ml whole milk)

8cm (3in) round cutter

A traditional recipe with a dark, spicy dough that must be kept as cold as possible with as little handling as you can manage. Be sure to chill it overnight, as this relaxes everything and allows the spices and molasses to develop and improve the flavour.

1. Using a freestanding electric mixer with the paddle attachment or a hand-held electric whisk, mix the butter, spices, salt, sugar, molasses and egg together and beat thoroughly for about 3 minutes.
2. Sift the flour into a bowl with the bicarbonate of soda, then add to the butter mixture and mix well. Add the sour milk and beat for a minute or two to mix together.
3. Bring the mixture together into a dough. Don't handle it too much and keep your hands cold and dry. Wrap the dough with cling film and chill overnight. The dough will be soft.
4. Preheat the oven to 190°C (375°F), Gas mark 5. Line two large baking sheets with non-stick baking parchment.
5. Divide the dough into four pieces. Refrigerate the dough that you are not immediately using. Roll out each piece on a well-floured surface to 5mm (¼in) thick and cut the cookies out with an 8cm (3in) round cutter. The dough is a little sticky, so flour well, then brush off any excess flour with a soft brush before baking. Reroll the dough each time until all the dough is used up. The dough will keep well in the fridge, wrapped in cling film, if you prefer to bake in batches.
6. Place the cookies onto the prepared baking sheets, leaving 5cm (2in) between them, and bake for about 8 minutes until the cookies have risen slightly and are spongy to touch. Allow to cool on the trays for 5 minutes, then transfer to a wire rack to cool completely.

Peanut Butter and Marshmallow Cookies

Makes 24 cookies

115g (4oz) unsalted butter,
   softened
110g (4oz) caster sugar
100g (3½oz) soft light
   brown sugar
1 large egg
125g (4½oz) peanut butter,
   smooth or crunchy,
   depending on taste
165g (6oz) plain flour
¾ tsp bicarbonate of soda
¼ tsp salt
¼ tsp baking powder
50g (1¾oz) mini
   marshmallows or
   chopped larger
   marshmallows

Peanut butter and marshmallows go so well together in these chewy cookies. Depending on your tastes, crunchy peanut butter can be used if you want added bite to your cookies. We've made these with white marshmallows, but you can also mix it up a little by adding some pink ones for extra colour.

1. Preheat the oven to 175°C (350°F), Gas mark 4. Line three large baking sheets with non-stick baking parchment.
2. Using a freestanding electric mixer with the paddle attachment or a hand-held electric whisk, cream the butter and sugars together for around 5 minutes on a medium-high speed until light and fluffy.
3. Add the egg and peanut butter to the mixture and beat for a further 2 minutes. Sift together the dry ingredients and add them to the butter and sugar mixture. Beat on a lower speed for a few moments until all is incorporated, scraping down the sides of the bowl as you go. Fold in the marshmallows by hand.
4. Using a tablespoon, form the cookie dough into balls (weighing about 30g (1oz) each). Place these balls of dough on the prepared baking sheets, leaving 5cm (2in) between them.
5. Bake the cookies for 11–13 minutes. Cool for 5 minutes before removing to a wire rack to cool completely.

Black Pepper Cookies

Makes 24–30 cookies

200g (7oz) soft light brown
  sugar
2 large eggs
180g (6½oz) plain flour
½ tsp salt
1 tsp ground cinnamon
½ tsp ground cloves
½ tsp ground black pepper
½ tsp bicarbonate
  of soda
½ tsp baking powder
90g (3oz) raisins
80g (3oz) chopped pecans

The recipe for these cookies comes from Maryland, one of the Mid-Atlantic states. The ground black pepper in the dough gives a certain edge to the cookies, slightly aromatic and only a little bit peppery. As with all cookies, the longer you bake them the crunchier and more brittle they become.

1. Preheat the oven to 175°C (350°F), Gas mark 4. Line three large baking sheets with non-stick baking parchment.
2. Using a freestanding electric mixer with the whisk attachment or a hand-held electric whisk, whisk the sugar and eggs until light and fluffy.
3. In a bowl, sift the flour, salt, spices, bicarbonate of soda and baking powder together and then add to the eggs and sugar, mixing until combined. Stir in the raisins and nuts by hand.
4. Measure out tablespoon-sized batches of dough onto the baking sheets, leaving 3cm (1¼in) between them.
5. Bake for 6–8 minutes, then cool for 5 minutes before removing to a wire rack to cool completely.

Black and White Cookies

Makes 12 cookies

For the cookies
270g (9½oz) plain flour
¼ tsp baking powder
¼ tsp salt
110g (4oz) unsalted butter,
  at room temperature
185g (6½oz) caster sugar
1 large egg, at room
  temperature
¼ tsp vanilla extract
¼ tsp lemon extract
115ml (4fl oz) whole milk

For the glaze
25g (1oz) dark chocolate
  (minimum 70% cocoa
  solids), finely chopped
40ml (1½fl oz) water
¼ tsp vanilla extract
30g (1oz) golden syrup
310g (11oz) icing sugar,
  sifted

Unlike most of the goodies in the book, these cookies aren't from the South, instead calling New York City their home. No Manhattan bakery would be complete without these half-chocolate, half-vanilla glazed cookies. Take time when putting on the glazes.

1. To make the cookies, preheat the oven to 190°C (375°F), Gas mark 5. Line two large baking sheets with non-stick baking parchment.
2. In a large bowl, mix together the flour, baking powder and salt with a fork or whisk and set aside.
3. Using a freestanding electric mixer with the paddle attachment or a hand-held electric whisk, beat the butter for 2 minutes on a low-medium speed until soft and fluffy. Slowly add the caster sugar, turn up the speed of the mixer and cream together for at least 2–3 minutes until the mixture is light in colour and fluffy.
4. Scrape down the sides of the bowl and add the egg and vanilla and lemon extracts, making sure you only beat until just incorporated. Add the flour mixture, on medium speed, alternating with the milk, in three additions. Only beat until each addition is just incorporated – don't overbeat. Scrape down the sides of the bowl between additions. Once everything has been incorporated, use a rubber spatula or spoon to stir by hand, making sure everything has been mixed in.
5. Spoon out 60g/2oz pieces of the dough (about 2 tablespoons per cookie) onto the prepared baking sheets, about 5cm (2in) apart. With wet fingers, press down the mounds into circles about 6cm (2½in) in diameter.
6. Bake the cookies for 15–17 minutes until light golden brown. Let them cool on the sheets for a couple of minutes, then put onto wire racks to cool completely.
7. To make the glaze, melt the dark chocolate in the microwave at medium strength in short increments (20 seconds maximum) until it's just melted. Alternatively, melt in a medium-sized glass heatproof bowl set over, but not touching, a pan of simmering water. Once melted, set aside.

▼

8. In a saucepan over a medium-high heat, bring the water, vanilla and golden syrup to a boil. Remove from the heat and quickly and briskly whisk in the sifted icing sugar. Transfer about 85g (3oz) of the vanilla icing to the bowl with the melted chocolate and whisk together until smooth – it will thicken considerably.

9. To glaze the cookies, it's best to place some greaseproof paper under the wire racks to catch any drips. Using an angled palette knife, spread about 1 teaspoon vanilla glaze onto half of each cookie, starting in the middle with a clean line. The glaze should be soft enough to spread when you tilt the cookies. Scrape round the edges to keep them glaze-free. Set aside to harden for at least 15 minutes. If the glaze gets too thick, you can stir in 1 teaspoon warm water at a time to loosen it.

10. Repeat on the other half of each cookie with the chocolate glaze, again loosening the mix by adding ½ teaspoon warm water at a time if you need to. Allow the cookies to set for about an hour until the glaze is hard.

Vanilla-filled Chocolate Cookies

**Makes 25–30
filled cookies**

For the cookies

170g (6oz) plain flour
90g (3oz) cocoa powder
1 tsp bicarbonate of soda
¼ tsp baking powder
¼ tsp salt
140g (5oz) unsalted butter,
 softened
320g (11oz) caster sugar,
 plus 3 tbsp extra
1 large egg

For the vanilla filling

225g (8oz) unsalted butter,
 softened
435g (15½oz) icing sugar
1 tbsp vanilla extract

Piping bag

These are a homemade version of a certain famous American
cookie! Be sure to press down the unbaked balls of dough with
the bottom of a glass dipped in caster sugar to prevent them
from sticking.

1. Preheat the oven to 190°C (375°F), Gas mark 5. Line three baking
sheets with baking parchment.
2. To make the cookies, sift the flour, cocoa, bicarbonate of soda,
baking powder and salt into a bowl.
3. Using a freestanding electric mixer with the paddle attachment
or a hand-held electric whisk, cream the butter and sugar together
for 5 minutes until light and fluffy. Add the egg and beat on medium
speed until just incorporated. Lower the speed and add the dry
ingredients gradually until the dough is well combined.
4. Using a small 15ml (½oz) scoop or a teaspoon, drop round dough

balls (weighing about 15g/½oz each) onto the baking sheets about
5cm (2in) apart. Press the bottom of a glass into a bowl of caster
sugar and use it to flatten the cookie dough to 3–4mm (about ⅛in)
thick. Be careful when removing the glass from the dough – use a
palette knife.

5. Bake for approximately 10 minutes until the cookies are firm.
Transfer to wire racks and cool completely.

6. To make the filling, using a freestanding mixer with the paddle
attachment or an electric whisk, beat the butter until it's light and
fluffy. On low speed, carefully add the icing sugar and when it's
just incorporated, turn up the speed and beat for 3 minutes until
light and fluffy. Add the vanilla and continue to beat for at least
2 more minutes.

7. To assemble the cookies, put the vanilla filling into a piping bag
and pipe about 1 tablespoon of the filling onto one of the cookies in
a spiral, leaving a little space around the edges. Cover with another
cookie and gently press together so that the filling now squeezes
out near the edges of the cookies. Repeat until you have used up
all the cookies and filling.

Cornmeal Cookies

Makes about 40 cookies

170g (6oz) unsalted butter,
   softened
160g (5½oz) caster sugar
1 large egg
200g (7oz) plain flour
1 tsp baking powder
¼ tsp salt
85g (3oz) yellow cornmeal
   (polenta)
1 tsp vanilla extract

These simple to make and delicious cookies come from a family recipe that was kindly given to us by author Donna Tartt. Her grandmother and great-grandmother used to make them, in Mississippi, and they use yellow cornmeal to give a crunchy texture. American cornmeal can be found online, or you can use polenta as an easy substitute.

1. Preheat the oven to 175°C (350°F), Gas mark 4. Line three large baking sheets with non-stick baking parchment.
2. Using a freestanding electric mixer with the paddle attachment or a hand-held electric whisk, cream the butter and sugar together for around 5 minutes on a medium-high speed until light and fluffy.
3. Beat in the egg, on a lower speed, scraping down the sides of the bowl as you go. In a bowl, sift the flour, baking powder and salt together and add to the creamed mixture. Add the cornmeal and vanilla and continue to beat on a medium speed until well mixed.
4. Drop 15g (½oz) teaspoon-sized batches of the dough from a spoon onto the prepared baking sheets, leaving about 5cm (2in) between them. Bake the cookies for about 10–12 minutes until golden. Leave to cool for 5 minutes on the baking sheets, then lift carefully with a palette knife onto a wire rack to cool completely.

Pumpkin and White Chocolate Cookies

Makes about 32 cookies

115g (4oz) unsalted butter,
  softened
110g (4oz) caster sugar
100g (3½oz) soft light
  brown sugar
1 large egg
½ tsp vanilla extract
220g (8oz) tinned pumpkin
  purée (such as Libby's)
270g (9½oz) plain flour
1 tsp bicarbonate of soda
½ tsp salt
1 tsp ground cinnamon
½ tsp ground ginger
¼ tsp ground nutmeg
¼ tsp ground cloves
170g (6oz) white chocolate
  chips

We tried a version of these cookies at a North Carolina bakery, and when you bite into them, they just taste like America. You could say they're a pumpkin spice latte in cookie form. They should remain soft, so don't bake them too long, and white chocolate seems to work better than dark or milk.

1. Preheat the oven to 175°C (350°F), Gas mark 4. Line three large baking sheets with non-stick baking parchment.
2. Using a freestanding electric mixer with the paddle attachment or a hand-held electric whisk, cream the butter and sugars together for around 5 minutes on a medium-high speed until light and fluffy.
3. Beat in the egg on a lower speed, scraping down the sides of the bowl as you go, followed by the vanilla extract and pumpkin purée, making sure everything is combined.
4. In a large bowl, sift all the remaining ingredients, except the chocolate chips, together. Slowly beat into the batter in thirds. Finally, fold in the white chocolate chips.
5. Measure out 30g (1oz) tablespoon-sized batches of dough onto the baking sheets, leaving 3cm (1¼in) between them. Press down on each ball of dough very gently with wet fingers to flatten slightly.
6. Bake for 12–14 minutes, until browned round the edges but soft inside. Cool for 5 minutes before removing to a wire rack to cool completely.

Lemon Drops

Makes 25 cookies

115g (4oz) unsalted butter,
  softened
Zest of 2 lemons
215g (7½oz) caster sugar
1 large egg
60ml (2fl oz) fresh
  lemon juice
60ml (2fl oz) cold water
270g (9½oz) plain flour
2 tsp baking powder
¼ tsp salt

These are quick to whip up and come out very soft and slightly spongy – it's easy to eat quite a lot of them in one sitting! As you're adding lemon juice to a buttery mixture, the mixture will look quite curdled until you add the dry ingredients, so don't worry.

1. Preheat the oven to 175°C (350°F), Gas mark 4. Line three large baking sheets with non-stick baking parchment.
2. Using a freestanding electric mixer with the paddle attachment or a hand-held electric whisk, cream the butter, lemon zest and sugar together for around 5 minutes on a medium-high speed until light and fluffy.
3. Add the egg, lemon juice and water to the butter mix and combine together on a low speed. The mixture will look slightly curdled, but that's fine. Sift the dry ingredients together in a bowl and add to the creamed mixture. Mix further with a spatula to make sure all is well mixed, but not overbeaten.
4. Measure out 30g (1oz) rounded tablespoon-sized pieces of cookie batter onto the baking sheets, leaving 3cm (1¼in) between them.
5. Bake for 12–14 minutes, then cool for 5 minutes before removing carefully to a wire rack to cool completely.

Birthday Cake Cookies

Makes 10–12 filled cookies or 20–24 unfilled

For the cookies
120g (4oz) unsalted butter,
   softened
200g (7oz) caster sugar
2 large egg yolks
1 tsp butter extract
   (can be bought online)
190g (7oz) plain flour
½ tsp baking powder
½ tsp salt
130g (4½oz) sprinkles, plus
   80g (3oz) extra for rolling

For the frosting (optional)
115g (4oz) unsalted butter,
   softened
1 tsp vanilla extract
Pinch of salt
375g (13oz) icing sugar
2-3 tbsp whole milk

Piping bag

Birthday cake flavoured goodies are all the rage in America, from M&Ms to ice cream to cookies. This simply means that the resulting sweet treat tastes like a traditional American vanilla birthday cake. Adding the butter extract gives that 'cake' flavour to these cookies.

1. Preheat the oven to 175°C (350°F), Gas mark 4. Line three baking sheets with non-stick baking parchment.
2. Using a freestanding electric mixer with the paddle attachment or a hand-held electric whisk, cream the butter and sugar together for around 5 minutes on a medium-high speed until light and fluffy.
3. Add the egg yolks, one at a time, making sure to scrape down the sides of the bowl between additions. Mix in the butter extract. Sift together the flour, baking powder and salt and add to the creamed mixture, combining gradually on a low speed. Fold through the sprinkles.
4. Roll the dough into approximately 30g (1oz) tablespoon-sized balls and place them on the prepared baking sheets, leaving about 5cm (2in) between them. Bake for about 9 minutes. Make sure they do not brown and take them out once the tops are firm and the gloss has gone. Allow to cool on the sheets for 5 minutes and then transfer to a wire rack to cool completely while you make the frosting.
5. Using a freestanding electric mixer with the paddle attachment or a hand-held electric whisk, beat the butter and vanilla together for about 5 minutes on a medium-high speed until light and creamy. Add the salt and beat for another minute.
6. Add the icing sugar a third at a time, on a low speed, and when it's mixed in, turn up the speed to medium. Add the milk 1 tablespoon at a time, turning the speed to high and beating for at least 5 minutes until very light and fluffy. Two tablespoons should be enough, but you may need one extra.
7. To assemble the cookies, put the frosting into a piping bag. Put the remaining 80g (3oz) sprinkles onto a flat tray or plate.
8. Pipe onto the bottom (flat side) of one of the cookies, starting at the edge and working inwards to the centre. Take another cookie and press the bottom (flat side) onto the frosting, sandwiching them together so a little of the frosting bulges out of the sides. Roll the exposed frosting onto the remaining sprinkles to decorate. Repeat with the remaining cookies.

Turtle Cookies

Makes 15 cookies

For the cookies
200g (7oz) plain flour
½ tsp bicarbonate of soda
½ tsp baking powder
¼ tsp salt
110g (4oz) unsalted butter,
  softened
100g (3½oz) soft
  light brown sugar
1 large egg, separated
½ tsp vanilla extract
100g (3½oz) pecan halves

For the frosting
60g (2oz) unsalted butter
30g (1oz) very dark
  chocolate (90–99%
  cocoa solids, such
  as Lindt Excellence)
80ml (3fl oz) whole milk
1 tsp vanilla extract
375g (13oz) icing sugar

One look at the picture will let you know why these New Orleans treats are called turtles! Using the darkest chocolate you can find will make your frosting more authentic – 100% baking chocolate is a common ingredient in the USA.

1. To make the cookies, preheat the oven to 190°C (375°F), Gas mark 5. Line two large baking sheets with non-stick baking parchment.
2. Sift the flour, bicarbonate of soda, baking powder and salt into a bowl. Set aside.
3. Using a freestanding electric mixer with the paddle attachment or a hand-held electric whisk, cream the butter and sugar together for around 5 minutes on a medium-high speed until light and fluffy.
4. In small bowls, beat the egg yolk and white separately by hand until loosened and slightly whipped. Add the egg yolk and vanilla to the creamed butter, followed by the dry ingredients, and beat on a low speed until well incorporated. Finally, add the egg white
5. Place three pecan halves very close together on a lined baking sheet. Around a centre point, two of the halves will stick out and look like legs and the third will be the turtle's head!
6. Take a 30g (1oz) tablespoon-sized batch of dough and roll into a rough ball, place on top of the pecans and slightly press down on the dough. Do the same until all the pecans and dough are used up, spacing each set of pecans 3–4cm (about 1½in) apart.
7. Bake the cookies for 12–15 minutes until light brown on the edges. Allow to cool while you make the frosting.
8. Put the butter, chocolate and milk in a saucepan and melt over a low heat (it will look curdled until everything is melted). Let this mixture cool to room temperature, and then stir in the vanilla. Sift the icing sugar into the bowl of a freestanding electric mixer with the paddle attachment or use a hand-held electric whisk. Add the melted chocolate mixture and beat until smooth and thickened. Top each cookie with a tablespoon of the frosting, smoothing the frosting with the back of a spoon.

Pumpkin Caramels

Makes 40–50 small squares

320g (11oz) caster sugar
60ml (2fl oz) water
60g (2oz) golden syrup
120ml (4fl oz) whipping
    cream
150g (5½oz) tinned
    pumpkin purée
    (such as Libby's)
60g (2oz) unsalted butter
¼ tsp salt
¼ tsp ground cinnamon
⅛ tsp ground allspice
⅛ tsp ground ginger
⅛ tsp ground nutmeg
½ tsp vanilla extract
Sea salt, for sprinkling
    (optional)

One 20 x 10cm (8 x 4in) loaf tin, Pyrex or metal dish and a sugar thermometer

Making caramels can seem daunting, as it's all about heating the sugar to the correct temperature. While experienced bakers in the past just knew when the mix looked right, using a sugar thermometer is indispensable here. Don't be tempted to stir your mixture at the beginning, or your sugar will crystallise and make everything very grainy.

1. Line the loaf tin, Pyrex or metal dish with baking parchment.
2. Place the sugar, water and syrup in a large saucepan – do not stir together. Simmer over a low heat for about 10 minutes until the sugar has dissolved. Again, don't stir during this process otherwise you risk crystallising the caramel. It will eventually dissolve on its own.
3. While the sugar is cooking, heat the cream, pumpkin purée, butter, salt and all the spices together in a saucepan until melted. Once the sugar syrup has turned to an amber colour, remove from the heat and slowly and carefully pour the pumpkin cream mixture into the bubbling amber sugar mixture. The liquid will bubble up a lot when adding the pumpkin cream, so be careful!
4. Return the pan to a low heat and cook for about 10 minutes until it reaches 110°C (230°F), measured on a sugar thermometer, add the vanilla, then continue to heat until it reaches soft ball stage, 120°C (248°F). Immediately pour the liquid caramel into the parchment-lined tin. Sprinkle the top with sea salt, if desired.
5. Cool for a few hours at room temperature until hard enough to cut into squares with a large sharp knife.

Creamy Pecan Pralines

Makes 25–30 pralines

180g (6½oz) chopped
   pecans
200g (7oz) soft light brown
   sugar
110g (4oz) caster sugar
120ml (4fl oz) whipping
   cream
60g (2oz) unsalted butter
2 tbsp water
¼ tsp salt

Sugar thermometer

Pralines originate in New Orleans and can be either plain or creamy.
We love the creamy ones as they're slightly chewier and have a
more fudgy taste. Stirring as little as possible will ensure that your
pralines are smooth and have no sugar crystals left when cooled.
Again, a sugar thermometer is a must.

1. Line three large baking sheets with non-stick baking parchment.
2. Toast the pecans by putting them in a dry frying pan over a
medium heat. This should only take 30–60 seconds; be careful
not to burn them.
3. Put the light brown sugar, caster sugar, whipping cream, butter,
water and salt into a saucepan. Stir once or twice only to mix
the ingredients.
4. Cook over a low heat until the sugar dissolves, only stirring
occasionally, then cook over a medium heat until the mixture
reaches soft ball stage, about 120°C (248°F), measured on a
sugar thermometer.
5. Remove the saucepan from the heat and stir in the pecans,
being careful as the mixture can thicken very quickly as it cools.
6. Drop pralines by the tablespoonful, using a teaspoon to help,
2.5cm (1in) apart onto the prepared baking sheets. Leave to cool
completely until firm.

Divinity

Makes about 30 candies

1 large egg white
60g (2oz) chopped pecans
30 pecan halves,
   to garnish
270g (9½oz) caster sugar
60ml (2fl oz) water
60ml (2fl oz) light corn
   syrup (or golden syrup)
Pinch of salt
½ tsp vanilla extract

Sugar thermometer

Even the name of these candies sounds Southern, and a well-made Divinity traditionally showed off the expertise and skill of the cook, as they're hard to make in the humid Southern climate. Read the recipe through a few times so that you can work as quickly as possible to form the rounded sweets once you've mixed everything up.

1. Line two large baking sheets with non-stick baking parchment.
2. Using a freestanding electric mixer with the whisk attachment or a hand-held electric whisk, beat the egg white on high speed until stiff peaks form.
3. Toast the chopped and halved pecans separately by putting them in a dry frying pan over a medium heat. This should only take 30–60 seconds; be careful not to burn them.
4. Mix the caster sugar, water, syrup and salt in a saucepan. Stir once or twice only to mix the ingredients. Cook over a low heat, only stirring occasionally, for about 15 minutes until the sugar dissolves and the mixture reaches about 125°C (257°F), hard ball stage, measured on a sugar thermometer.
5. Remove the syrup mixture from the heat and very carefully pour in a thin stream over the whisked egg white, beating constantly at high speed, until all the syrup has been incorporated and the mixture is stiff, glossy and holding its shape. Stir in the vanilla and the chopped pecans.
6. Working quickly, drop rounded teaspoons of the mixture onto the prepared baking sheets. Garnish with pecan halves and leave to cool.

Traybakes

Lemon Crumb Squares
Coconut Dream Bars
Red Velvet Brownies
Pumpkin Hazelnut Bars
Caramel Chocolate Chip
  Cookie Bars
Blackberry Limeade Bars
Texas Tassie Bars
Chocolate Carrot Brownies
Pear Treasure Squares

Lemon Crumb Squares

**Makes one 23 x 32cm
(9 x 13in) tray, to slice
as desired**

For the base and topping

180g (6½oz) plain flour
½ tsp salt
1 tsp baking powder
115g (4oz) unsalted butter,
    softened
200g (7oz) soft dark
    brown sugar
90g (3oz) rolled oats

For the filling

370ml (12½fl oz) sweet
    condensed milk
140ml (5fl oz) fresh lemon
    juice
Zest of 1 lemon

One 23 x 32cm (9 x 13in) tin

These tangy treats are so easy to make. Although they are put into
the fridge for about an hour after cooling, they'll still be soft, gooey
and wonderful. You can bake a couple of minutes longer if you want
your topping to be crunchier, but keep an eye on them in the oven,
as you don't want to dry out the filling too much.

1. Preheat the oven to 175°C (350°F), Gas mark 4. Line the tin with
non-stick baking parchment.
2. To make the base and topping, sift the flour, salt and baking
powder together into a bowl and set aside.
3. Using a freestanding electric mixer with the paddle attachment
or a hand-held electric whisk, cream the butter and sugar together
for around 5 minutes on a medium-high speed until light and fluffy.
Add the oats and the flour mixture to the butter and sugar and mix
until it resembles breadcrumbs.
4. Press half of this mixture into the base of the prepared tin and
set the rest aside in a bowl.
5. To make the filling, in the bowl of a freestanding electric mixer
with the whisk attachment or using a hand-held electric whisk,
whisk together the condensed milk, lemon juice and zest.
6. To assemble, spread the filling evenly onto the pressed base.
Sprinkle the rest of the reserved topping gently over the filling.
7. Bake for 20–25 minutes until the topping begins to go brown.
Cool at room temperature for 30 minutes and then in the fridge
for at least 1 hour. Cut into the desired-size slices.

Coconut Dream Bars

Makes one 23 x 32cm (9 x 13in) tray, to slice as desired

For the base
200g (7oz) unsalted
  butter, softened
180g (6½oz) soft light
  brown sugar
360g (12½oz) plain flour

For the topping
4 large eggs
350g (12oz) soft light
  brown sugar
¾ tsp baking powder
30g (1oz) plain flour
½ tsp salt
250g (9oz) desiccated
  coconut
100g (3½oz) chopped
  pecans or walnuts
1¾ tsp vanilla extract

One 23 x 32cm (9 x 13in) tin

The reason these are called dream bars will become obvious as soon as you bite into one. You could use another type of nut or a mix of different nuts, according to your tastes, but keep the total weight the same as in the recipe. We've left it up to you to decide how many slices you'd like to cut!

1. Preheat the oven to 175°C (350°F), Gas mark 4. Line the tin with non-stick baking parchment.
2. To make the base, using a freestanding electric mixer with the paddle attachment or a hand-held electric whisk, cream the butter and sugar together for around 5 minutes on a medium-high speed until light and fluffy. Add the flour and mix well.
3. Spread the mixture into the base of the tin using the back of a spoon. Bake for 10 minutes, then remove from the oven and set aside to cool while you prepare the topping.
4. To make the topping, using a freestanding electric mixer with the whisk attachment or a hand-held electric whisk, beat the eggs, brown sugar, baking powder, flour and salt until well mixed. Stir in the coconut and nuts by hand, along with the vanilla extract.
5. Pour the topping over the baked layer and put back into the oven for 15 minutes or until the topping has set. Remove from the oven and allow to cool before cutting into your desired-size slices.

Red Velvet Brownies

**Makes one 23 x 32cm
(9 x 13in) tray, to slice
as desired**

For the brownie layer
200g (7oz) unsalted butter
390g (13½oz) caster sugar
2 tsp vanilla extract
55g (2oz) cocoa powder
1 tsp red gel paste
    colouring, mixed
    with water to make
    1½ tbsp liquid
2 tsp white vinegar
4 large eggs
175g (6oz) plain flour
½ tsp salt

**For the cream cheese
layer**
390g (13½oz) full-fat
    cream cheese such as
    Philadelphia, softened
100g (3½oz) caster sugar
2 large eggs
½ tsp vanilla extract

One 23 x 32cm (9 x 13in) tin

We're sure you've wondered, just as we often have, what would happen if brownies were mixed with Red Velvet cake? The result will definitely please the Red Velvet lovers out there. And these brownies don't just taste amazing, but look great too, so be sure to get creative with your cream cheese topping swirling techniques!

1. Preheat the oven to 175°C (350°F), Gas mark 4. Line the tin with non-stick baking parchment.
2. To make the brownie layer, melt the butter in a medium-sized heatproof glass bowl set over, but not touching, a pan of simmering water, then stir in the caster sugar and vanilla. Beat by hand until the mix is slightly thickened, then remove from the heat.
3. Using a freestanding electric mixer with the paddle attachment or a hand-held electric whisk, mix the cocoa powder, red food colouring and vinegar with the sugar and butter mixture and beat until incorporated. Add the eggs and beat until nice and smooth, then fold in the flour and salt.
4. Pour the red velvet batter into the prepared tin, saving about 60ml (2fl oz) of the batter for the top and setting this aside.
5. To make the cream cheese layer, beat together the cream cheese, sugar, eggs and vanilla extract until smooth.
6. Spread the cream cheese over the *raw* red velvet layer, carefully smoothing it evenly. Dollop bits of the reserved red velvet batter onto the cream cheese layer and, using a skewer, swirl to make patterns.
7. Bake for about 30–35 minutes, or until the top is firm to the touch and just starting to go golden at the edges. Remove from the oven and allow to cool before cutting.

Pumpkin Hazelnut Bars

**Makes one 23 x 32cm
(9 x 13in) tray, to slice
as desired**

For the crust
115g (4oz) unsalted butter,
   softened
70g (2½oz) caster sugar
235g (8½oz) plain flour

For the filling
215g (7½oz) caster sugar
2 large eggs
425g (15oz) tinned pumpkin
   purée (such as Libby's)
455g (1lb) full-fat
cream cheese, such as
   Philadelphia, softened
1 tsp vanilla extract
½ tsp ground nutmeg

For the topping
260g (9oz) hazelnuts,
   chopped
30g (1oz) unsalted butter,
   softened
100g (3½oz) soft dark
   brown sugar
2 tbsp plain flour
1 tsp ground cinnamon

One 23 x 32cm (9 x 13in) tin

There aren't too many Southern recipes calling for hazelnuts, so this one makes a nice change. Using tinned pumpkin in baking is second nature in the USA and strangely works better than trying to use fresh. You can substitute another type of nut, according to your tastes, if you like.

1. Preheat the oven to 175°C (350°F), Gas mark 4. Line the tin with non-stick baking parchment.
2. To make the crust, using a freestanding electric mixer with the paddle attachment or a hand-held electric whisk, cream the butter and sugar together for around 5 minutes on a medium-high speed until light and fluffy. Add the flour and mix well. Press the crust into the base of the prepared tin. Set aside.
3. To make the filling, in the bowl of a freestanding electric mixer with the paddle attachment or using a hand-held electric whisk, mix together all the filling ingredients and beat together just until smooth. Don't overbeat or the cream cheese will split and become runny. Pour the filling over the unbaked crust, even out with a spatula and set aside.
4. To make the topping, rub together all the topping ingredients with your fingertips to make a crumble mix. Spread evenly over the unbaked filling.
5. Bake for 50–60 minutes until the filling is firm. Allow to cool completely then chill before cutting into the desired-size slices.

Caramel Chocolate Chip Cookie Bars

Makes one 23 x 32cm (9 x 13in) tray, to slice as desired

350g (12oz) plain flour
1 tsp baking powder
¾ tsp salt
295g (10½oz) unsalted
  butter, softened
500g (1lb 2oz) soft light
  brown sugar
4 large eggs
2½ tsp vanilla extract
150g (5½oz) dark
  (minimum 70% cocoa
  solids) or milk chocolate
  chips
150g (5½oz) caramel bits
55ml (2fl oz) double
  cream

One 23 x 32cm (9 x 13in) tin

You can buy Caramel Bits online, or use any toffee or soft caramels instead, making sure you keep to the same weight as asked for in the recipe. These are a lovely traybake version of chocolate chip cookies, with a very welcome caramel twist.

1. Preheat the oven to 175°C (350°F), Gas mark 4. Line the tin with non-stick baking parchment.
2. Sift the flour, baking powder and salt together into a bowl and set aside.
3. Using a freestanding electric mixer with the paddle attachment or a hand-held electric whisk, cream the butter and sugar together for around 5 minutes on a medium-high speed until light and fluffy.
4. Add the eggs, one at a time, scraping down the sides of the bowl after each addition, then add the vanilla extract. Turn the speed to low and add the flour mixture in small amounts until just incorporated. Stir in the chocolate chips. Spread the batter into the prepared tin and set aside.
5. Place the caramel bits with the cream in a small heatproof mixing bowl. Put the bowl over, but not touching, a pan of simmering water and allow the caramel to melt, stirring often. Pour the melted caramel over the batter and even out with a spatula.
6. Bake for 30 minutes until a skewer inserted in the centre comes out clean. The bars will rise and fall while baking. Cool for at least 1 hour before cutting.

Blackberry Limeade Bars

Makes one 23 x 32cm (9 x 13in) tray, to slice as desired

For the base

195g (7oz) unsalted butter, softened
95g (3½oz) caster sugar
235g (8oz) plain flour
½ tsp salt

For the filling

560g (1lb 3oz) caster sugar
120g (4oz) plain flour
9 limes, 2 zested and all juiced to yield 270ml (10fl oz) juice
½ tsp salt
2 large eggs
5 large egg whites
400g (14oz) blackberries (if using frozen, defrost first)

One 23 x 32cm (9 x 13in) tin

The purplish hue of these bars is so striking and there's no food colouring involved, thanks to the blackberries! If the berries aren't in season or you're on a tight budget, frozen will do, as will bottled lime juice.

1. Preheat the oven to 175°C (350°F), Gas mark 4. Line the tin with non-stick baking parchment.
2. To make the base, using a freestanding electric mixer with the paddle attachment or a hand-held electric whisk, cream the butter and sugar together for around 5 minutes on a medium-high speed until light and smooth. Add the flour and salt and mix until everything is well combined.
3. Press the mixture into the base of the prepared tin using the back of a spoon. If it gets too sticky, dip the spoon in some flour to help push the dough down.
4. Bake for 15 minutes until lightly golden. Remove from the oven and set aside to cool while you prepare the filling.
5. Using a freestanding electric mixer with the whisk attachment or a hand-held electric whisk, mix together the sugar, flour, lime zest, salt, whole eggs and egg whites.
6. Put the blackberries into a food processor or hand blender and process until very smooth. Put this purée through a fine sieve, discarding the pips, and add to the rest of the filling mixture. Whisk in the lime juice and mix everything together until smooth and well incorporated.
7. Pour the filling over the baked crust and put back in the oven to cook for 25–30 minutes until the centre has set when the dish is wiggled. Remove from the oven and cool for 30 minutes at room temperature, then cover the top with cling film and cool in the fridge for at least 2 hours. Once fully cooled, cut into the desired-size slices with a large sharp knife.

Texas Tassie Bars

Makes one 23 x 32cm (9 x 13in) tray, to slice as desired

For the crust
250g (9oz) plain flour
120g (4oz) soft light brown sugar
½ tsp baking powder
200g (7oz) unsalted butter, softened
60g (2oz) chopped pecans

For the filling
120g (4oz) soft dark brown sugar
50g (1¾oz) plain flour
4 large eggs, lightly beaten
160g (5½oz) golden syrup
160g (5½oz) treacle
2 tsp vanilla extract
1 tbsp Kentucky bourbon or whiskey (optional)
½ tsp salt
220g (8oz) chopped pecans

One 23 x 32cm (9 x 13in) tin

In Texas, a pecan tassie is a type of mini pecan pie and, indeed, the state tree of Texas is the pecan itself. If you've ever wondered why so many American recipes use pecans, it's because they're native to the south-eastern and south-central USA. The gooey filling is divine, but please make sure it's fully cooled before biting in.

1. Preheat the oven to 175°C (350°F), Gas mark 4. Line the tin with non-stick baking parchment.
2. To make the crust, put the flour, brown sugar and baking powder in a bowl and mix well. Rub the butter into the flour and sugar with cold fingertips until crumbly. Add the pecans, mix well and press all the mixture into the base of the prepared tin.
3. Bake for 15 minutes, then remove from the oven and cool for 5–10 minutes while you make the filling.
4. In the bowl of a freestanding electric mixer with the paddle attachment or a bowl you can use a hand-held electric whisk in, mix together the brown sugar and flour by hand. Add the eggs, syrup, treacle, vanilla, bourbon (if using) and salt and beat to mix well. Carefully pour the filling over the baked crust and sprinkle with the remaining pecans.
5. Bake for 20–25 minutes until the topping has set. Cool for at least 2 hours before slicing.

Chocolate Carrot Brownies

**Makes one 23 x 32cm
(9 x 13in) tray, to slice
as desired**

400g (14oz) dark chocolate
   (minimum 70% cocoa
   solids), roughly chopped
200g (7oz) unsalted butter
150g (5½oz) plain flour
195g (7oz) caster sugar
2 tsp salt
5 large eggs
240g (8½oz) carrots,
   peeled and grated
175g (6oz) chopped pecans
   or walnuts
Grated zest of 1 orange
2 tsp vanilla extract
100g (3½oz) raisins

One 23 x 32cm (9 x 13in) tin

Another brownie variant to add to your growing repertoire,
but this time using carrots. They give these brownies a different
texture, as do the raisins and nuts. As with all brownies, the longer
you bake them, the less gooey and chewy they'll be when cooled,
so use your judgement when testing for doneness.

1. Preheat the oven to 175°C (350°F), Gas mark 4. Line the tin with
non-stick baking parchment.
2. Put the chocolate and butter in a small heatproof mixing bowl.
Put the bowl over, but not touching, a pan of simmering water and
stir so that the butter and chocolate melt and are mixed well, then
set aside.
3. Sift the flour, sugar and salt into a bowl. Set aside.
4. Using a freestanding electric mixer with the whisk attachment or
a hand-held electric whisk, beat the eggs together. Add the melted
chocolate and butter, followed by the flour and sugar, and mix until
well incorporated. Fold in the carrots, nuts, zest, vanilla and raisins
by hand.
5. Pour into the prepared tin and bake for about 20–25 minutes,
or until a skewer inserted into the centre comes out clean. The
brownies should cool in the tin until they reach room temperature
before cutting.

Pear Treasure Squares

**Makes one 23 x 32cm
(9 x 13in) tray, to slice
as desired**

415g (14½oz) tin pears,
  in natural juices
115g (4oz) unsalted butter,
  softened
150g (5½oz) soft light
  brown sugar
1 large egg
1 tsp vanilla extract
210g (7½oz) wholemeal
  flour
1 tsp bicarbonate of soda
½ tsp salt
½ tsp ground cinnamon
65g (2oz) chopped pecans
  or walnuts
175g (6oz) dark chocolate
  chips (minimum 70%
  cocoa solids)
175g (6oz) raisins
80g (3oz) dates, chopped

One 23 x 32cm (9 x 13in) tin

The treasures in these wholemeal bars are the little bites of pear, dark chocolate chips, raisins, dates and nuts within. You can of course use another type of tinned fruit, such as peaches, or another type of nut, or even milk chocolate chips, but make sure to keep the weight the same as in the recipe.

1. Preheat the oven to 175°C (350°F), Gas mark 4. Line the tin with non-stick baking parchment.
2. Over a bowl, drain the pears and reserve 120ml (4fl oz) of the liquid, discarding the rest. Dice the pears and set aside in a bowl.
3. Using a freestanding electric mixer with the paddle attachment or a hand-held electric whisk, cream the butter and sugar together for around 5 minutes on a medium-high speed until light and fluffy.
4. Add the egg, vanilla and pear juice and mix well. The mixture will look curdled at this stage. Sift together the flour, bicarbonate of soda, salt and cinnamon and mix into the creamed mixture until well incorporated. Stir in the nuts, chocolate chips, raisins, diced pear and dates by hand.
5. Pour the mixture into the prepared tin and bake for 30 minutes, until a skewer inserted into the cake comes out clean. Cool for 15 minutes and cut into bars while still warm.

Pancakes

Red Velvet Pancakes
Black Bottom Pancakes
Buttermilk Pancakes
Pumpkin Pancakes
Oatmeal Pancakes
Cinnamon Pancake Cake
Kentucky Apple Pancake
Sally Lunn French Toast

Red Velvet Pancakes

Makes 8 pancakes

For the pancakes
135g (5oz) plain flour
20g (¾oz) cocoa powder
1 tsp baking powder
¼ tsp bicarbonate of soda
¼ tsp salt
235ml (8fl oz) buttermilk
1 tbsp white vinegar (can
   be cider, wine or distilled)
55g (2oz) caster sugar
1 large egg
½ tsp red gel paste
   colouring mixed in
   1 tbsp water
1 tsp vanilla extract
35g (1¼oz) unsalted butter,
   melted
Vegetable oil, for the pan

**For the cream cheese
syrup**
80g (3oz) full-fat cream
   cheese, such as
   Philadelphia, softened
45g (1½oz) unsalted butter,
   softened
125g (4½oz) icing sugar
¼ tsp vanilla extract
60ml (2fl oz) whole milk,
   plus more if desired

With these beautiful pancakes, our affair with everything Red Velvet can start first thing in the morning! Keep an eye on them as they cook in the pan, as the longer they cook, the darker the colour will become.

1. To make the pancakes, in a mixing bowl whisk together the flour, cocoa, baking powder, bicarbonate of soda and salt by hand.
2. In a jug, mix the buttermilk and vinegar together and set aside for 2 minutes.
3. Pour the buttermilk and vinegar into a mixing bowl and add the caster sugar, egg, red colouring, vanilla and melted butter. Mix together until thoroughly combined. Slowly add the dry ingredients to the wet, mixing until the ingredients are just incorporated.
4. Put a non-stick frying pan on a low-medium heat. To make your first pancake, add a little vegetable oil to the pan so it doesn't stick, then spoon 4 tablespoons of the batter into the pan. Let the pancake cook, undisturbed, for 1–2 minutes until bubbles rise to the surface and the edges look dry. At that point, lift the underside up with a spatula to make sure it's nicely browned and flip over. Continue to cook for about 1 minute more until the second side is also nicely browned. Remove from the pan and place in a warm oven while you cook the rest of the pancakes.
5. To make the cream cheese syrup, using a freestanding electric mixer with the paddle attachment or a hand-held electric whisk combine the cream cheese and butter on a medium speed for about 2 minutes, until light and fluffy.
6. Add the rest of the ingredients on a lower speed, withholding some of the milk, and mix until well combined. Add more milk to thin out the mixture to your desired consistency. Pour the cream cheese syrup on top of the pancakes and enjoy.

Black Bottom Pancakes

Makes 4–5 pancakes

For the pancakes

135g (5oz) plain flour

2 tbsp cocoa powder

2 tbsp caster sugar

1 tbsp soft light brown sugar

1 tsp baking powder

½ tsp bicarbonate of soda

Pinch of salt

235ml (8fl oz) buttermilk

1 large egg

2 tbsp rapeseed or vegetable oil

1 tsp vanilla extract

85g (3oz) dark chocolate chips (minimum 70% cocoa solids)

Vegetable oil, for the pan

For the cream cheese syrup

85g (3oz) full-fat cream cheese, such as Philadelphia, softened

45g (1½oz) unsalted butter, softened

125g (4½oz) icing sugar

60ml (2fl oz) whole milk, plus more if desired

½ tsp vanilla extract

Black Bottom cupcakes needed a spin-off, so what could be better than double chocolate chip pancakes and cream cheese syrup? Remember, the first pancake never looks perfect, so you can eat that one yourself while cooking the rest!

1. To make the pancakes, in a large mixing bowl whisk together the flour, cocoa, caster sugar, brown sugar, baking powder, bicarbonate of soda and salt by hand.

2. In a separate bowl, whisk together the buttermilk, egg, oil and vanilla extract. Add the wet to the dry ingredients and fold in gently. Don't overmix – the batter should be lumpy and thick. Fold in the chocolate chips.

3. Put a non-stick frying pan on a low-medium heat. To make your first pancake, add a little vegetable oil to the pan so the pancake doesn't stick, then spoon 4 tablespoons of the batter into the pan. Let the pancake cook, undisturbed, for 1–2 minutes until bubbles rise to the surface and the edges look dry. At that point, lift the underside up with a spatula to make sure it's nicely browned and flip over. Continue to cook for about 1 minute more until the second side is also nicely browned. Remove from the pan and place in a warm oven while you cook the rest of the pancakes.

4. To make the cream cheese syrup, using a freestanding electric mixer with the paddle attachment or a hand-held electric whisk, combine the cream cheese and butter on medium speed for about 2 minutes, until light and fluffy.

5. Add the rest of the ingredients on a lower speed, withholding some of the milk, and mix until well combined. Add more milk to thin out the mixture to your desired consistency. Pour the cream cheese syrup on top of the hot pancakes and enjoy.

Buttermilk Pancakes

Makes 8 pancakes

45g (1½oz) unsalted butter
270g (9½oz) plain flour
55g (2oz) caster sugar
2½ tsp baking powder
½ tsp bicarbonate of soda
½ tsp salt
470ml (16½fl oz) buttermilk
2 large eggs
Handful of blueberries
   (optional)
Vegetable oil, for the pan
Maple syrup or lemon curd,
   to serve (optional)

These are the quintessential American pancakes you'd get in any diner worth its salt in the USA. Fluffy and airy, they're perfect for soaking up maple syrup. Along with eggs over easy and crispy bacon, no American breakfast is complete without them.

1. To make the pancakes, melt the butter in the microwave or in a small saucepan on the stove and set aside to cool briefly.
2. In a large bowl, whisk the flour, sugar, baking powder, bicarbonate of soda and salt together by hand.
3. In a separate bowl, whisk the buttermilk and eggs. Pour the wet ingredients into the dry ingredients and whisk gently by hand until the dry ingredients are almost incorporated; stop before the batter is evenly mixed – it should be lumpy. Fold in the blueberries, if using, but don't overmix.
4. Add the cooled melted butter and mix just until the batter is incorporated – it will still be lumpy. Let the batter rest while you heat a non-stick frying pan on a low heat.
5. To make your first pancake, add a little vegetable oil to the pan so it doesn't stick, then spoon 4 tablespoons of the batter into the pan. Let the pancake cook, undisturbed, for 1–2 minutes until bubbles rise to the surface and the edges look dry. At that point, lift the underside up with a spatula to make sure it's nicely browned and flip over. Continue to cook for about 1 minute more until the second side is also nicely browned. Remove from the pan and place in a warm oven while you cook the rest of the pancakes. Once all the pancakes are cooked, serve with maple syrup or lemon curd, if you like.

Pumpkin Pancakes

Makes 6 pancakes

30g (1oz) butter
170g (6oz) plain flour
2 tbsp soft light brown
   sugar
2 tsp baking powder
½ tsp ground cinnamon
½ tsp ground ginger
½ tsp ground nutmeg
¼ tsp allspice
¼ tsp ground cloves
½ tsp salt
235ml (8½fl oz)
   semi-skimmed milk
170g (6oz) tinned pumpkin
   purée (such as Libby's)
1 large egg
Vegetable oil, for the pan
Butter and maple syrup
   and chopped pecans,
   to serve (optional)

These pumpkin spice pancakes are perfect with your morning coffee, especially when the weather turns a bit colder and mornings are a bit darker. Using pumpkin purée in baked goods always gives them that extra richness and moisture, and it works perfectly with these fluffy pancakes, especially when they're smothered in maple syrup.

1. To make the pancakes, melt the butter in the microwave or in a small saucepan on the stove and set aside to cool briefly.
2. In a bowl, sift together the flour, sugar, baking powder, spices and salt.
3. In a separate bowl, whisk together the milk, pumpkin purée, melted butter and egg. Fold the wet ingredients gently into the dry ingredients.
4. Put a non-stick frying pan on a medium heat. To make your first pancake, add a little vegetable oil to the pan so it doesn't stick, then spoon 4 tablespoons of the batter into the pan. Let the pancake cook, undisturbed, for 1–2 minutes until bubbles rise to the surface and the edges look dry. At that point, lift the underside up with a spatula to make sure it's nicely browned and flip over. Continue to cook for about 1 minute more until the second side is also nicely browned. Remove from the pan and place in a warm oven while you cook the rest of the pancakes. Once all the pancakes are cooked, serve with butter and maple syrup and sprinkle with the pecans, if you like.

Oatmeal Pancakes

Makes 4 pancakes

65g (2oz) plain flour
50g (1¾oz) rolled oats
1 tbsp caster sugar
1 tsp baking powder
½ tsp bicarbonate of soda
½ tsp salt
175ml (6fl oz) buttermilk
1 tsp vanilla extract
2 tbsp vegetable oil
1 large egg
Vegetable oil, for the pan
Maple syrup or honey,
    to serve (optional)

If you thought America had only one kind of pancake, you're probably beginning to realise that you were wrong! Oatmeal pancakes feature on many restaurant breakfast menus down South, and they give a slightly different texture and flavour to plain flour pancakes. Serve with maple syrup or runny honey.

1. Blitz the flour and oats together in a food processor with the blade attachment until the oats are broken down to the consistency of a rough flour.
2. In a bowl, mix all the dry ingredients together.
3. In a separate bowl, whisk together the buttermilk, vanilla, oil and egg until smooth. Add the dry ingredients to the wet and stir to combine. Do not overmix.
4. Put a non-stick frying pan on a low-medium heat. To make your first pancake, add a little vegetable oil to the pan so it doesn't stick, then spoon 4 tablespoons of the batter into the pan. Let the pancake cook, undisturbed, for 1–2 minutes until bubbles rise to the surface and the edges look dry. At that point, lift the underside up with a spatula to make sure it's nicely browned and flip over. Continue to cook for about 1 minute more until the second side is also nicely browned. Remove from the pan and place in a warm oven while you cook the rest of the pancakes. Serve with maple syrup or honey, if you like.

Cinnamon Pancake Cake

Makes one 17.5cm (7in) cake, to slice as desired

For the pancake cake

135g (5oz) plain flour
40g (1½oz) wholemeal flour
25g (1oz) yellow cornmeal
   (polenta)
55g (2oz) caster sugar
2 tbsp soft light brown
   sugar
2 tsp baking powder
1 tsp ground cinnamon
½ tsp ground nutmeg
½ tsp salt
295ml (10fl oz) whole milk
2 large eggs
2 large egg yolks
30g (1oz) unsalted butter,
   melted
1 tsp vanilla extract

For the filling

315g (11oz) full-fat cream
   cheese, such as
   Philadelphia
60ml (2fl oz) full-fat
   Greek yoghurt
75ml (2½fl oz) maple syrup
30g (1oz) icing sugar
½ tsp ground cinnamon

Vegetable oil, for the pan
Handful of crushed pecans,
   to decorate (optional)

One 17.5cm (7in) non-stick frying pan

This pancake cake would make an impressive addition to any Sunday brunch. Although it can be served at other times of the day, adding crispy rashers of bacon in between the pancake layers will make this an American breakfast in one slice!

1. To make the pancakes, mix the plain flour, wholemeal flour, cornmeal, both sugars, baking powder, cinnamon, nutmeg and salt together in a bowl.

2. In a separate bowl, combine the milk, eggs, yolks, melted butter and vanilla extract and whisk well. Add the dry ingredients to the wet ingredients and mix. The batter may be lumpy, but don't worry if it is. Don't overmix.

3. Put the non-stick frying pan on a low-medium heat. To make your first pancake, add a little vegetable oil to the pan, then pour 120ml (4fl oz) of the batter into the pan. Let the pancake cook, undisturbed, for 3–4 minutes until bubbles rise to the surface and the edges look dry. At that point, lift the underside up with a spatula to make sure it's nicely browned and flip over. Continue to cook for about 1 minute more until the second side is also nicely browned. Repeat with the rest of the batter, until you've made another 5 pancakes.

4. To make the filling, in the bowl of a freestanding electric mixer with the paddle attachment or using a hand-held electric whisk, beat the cream cheese and yoghurt until smooth and well mixed. Add 60ml (2fl oz) of the maple syrup (leaving about 1 tablespoon behind) to the mix, then add the icing sugar and cinnamon mixing until all is well combined, but don't overbeat.

5. Wait until the pancakes have cooled slightly before assembling the cake. Spread some of the filling on top of one of the pancakes, spreading it evenly until most of the pancake is covered, leaving a ring round the edge unfilled. Put another pancake on top, spread with more filling and repeat until you've placed all six pancakes on top of each other. Finish with a final layer of filling on the top pancake. Pour the remaining 1 tablespoon of maple syrup over the top and sprinkle with crushed pecans, if desired.

Kentucky Apple Pancake

Makes a single 25cm (10in) pancake, to slice as desired.

75g (2½oz) plain flour
½ tsp baking powder
¼ tsp salt
55ml (1¾fl oz) fresh lemon juice
360g (12½oz) apples, peeled and cut into bite-sized pieces
6 large eggs, separated
100g (3½oz) soft light brown sugar
110g (4oz) caster sugar
130ml (4½fl oz) whole milk
2 tsp vanilla extract
55g (2oz) unsalted butter
1 tsp ground cinnamon
½ tsp ground nutmeg

One 25cm (10in) cast-iron skillet or ovenproof pan

This big pancake comes out of the oven like a fluffy soufflé. It does deflate as it cools, so don't worry, just cut or spoon it out into wedges as quickly as you can and serve it warm with some maple syrup, runny custard or jam.

1. Preheat the oven to 190°C (375°F), Gas mark 5.

2. Sift together the flour, baking powder and salt into a bowl and set aside.

3. Put the apple in a bowl and pour over the lemon juice.

4. Using a freestanding electric mixer with the whisk attachment or a hand-held electric whisk, beat the egg whites until foamy, then gradually add the brown and caster sugar, reserving 2 tablespoons of each, while beating, until the whites reach the stiff peak stage.

5. In a separate bowl, beat the egg yolks until thickened, then beat in the milk and vanilla extract.

6. Add the flour mixture to the egg yolk mixture and beat until smooth. Fold in the egg whites and the apple.

7. Melt the butter in the skillet or pan and pour in the pancake mixture. Sprinkle with the reserved caster and brown sugar and the cinnamon and nutmeg.

8. Bake for 25–30 minutes until the pancake is set and lightly browned. If the sugar top starts burning in the oven, put a metal baking sheet above it until the pancake is firm and has cooked through. Cut the pancake into wedges while still warm. It will deflate as it cools – this is normal, so serve quickly.

Sally Lunn French Toast

Serves 4

8 slices of Sally Lunn Loaf
  (see page 228) or brioche
  or thickly sliced white
  bread
2 large eggs
115ml (4fl oz) whole milk
115ml (4fl oz) single cream
Pinch of salt
1 tbsp caster sugar
1 tsp vanilla extract
1 tsp ground cinnamon
30g (1oz) unsalted butter

The Sally Lunn loaf that we show you how to make on page 228 makes the most perfect French toast; however, thick slices of brioche or white bread are great too. The trick is to soak your bread in the eggy mixture very thoroughly before cooking it in the frying pan.

1. Place four slices of Sally Lunn or other bread in a baking dish.
2. In a bowl, whisk together the eggs, milk, cream, salt, sugar, vanilla and cinnamon.
3. Pour half the liquid mixture over the four Sally Lunn slices in the baking dish. Allow to soak in.
4. Melt half the butter in a frying pan on a medium heat.
5. Put the soggy Sally Lunn slices in the hot frying pan and cook until golden brown on each side. Repeat the steps above with the remaining four slices of Sally Lunn and the rest of the egg and cream mixture.

Ice Cream

Buttermilk Ice Cream
Red Velvet Ice Cream
Grasshopper Pie Ice Cream
Pumpkin Ice Cream
Earl Grey Tea and Chocolate
    Ice Cream
South Carolina Fig Ice Cream
Fresh Peach Ice Cream
Peanut Butter Ice Cream
Lemon Custard Ice Cream

Buttermilk Ice Cream

**Makes 480ml (17fl oz)
ice cream**

235ml (8fl oz) double
    cream
135g (5oz) caster sugar
6 large egg yolks
235ml (8fl oz) buttermilk
1 tsp vanilla extract
Pinch of salt

Ice-cream maker

Buttermilk ice cream is like vanilla ice cream with a more
sophisticated layering of taste and a tangy kick. We would happily
eat scoops and scoops of it on its own, but it goes very nicely with
a slice of hot pie or hot bread pudding.

1. In a large, heavy saucepan, combine the double cream and 100g
(3½oz) of the sugar and bring to a simmer over a medium heat.
2. Using a freestanding electric mixer with the whisk attachment
or a hand-held electric whisk, whisk the egg yolks and remaining
sugar until the egg yolks have thickened and are slightly lighter
in colour.
3. Whisk half a cup of the hot cream mixture into the egg mixture
to warm it up, whisking constantly to keep the eggs from cooking.
Then slowly whisk the egg mixture into the rest of the cream mixture
in the saucepan. Stir the custard over a low heat until the mixture
is thick enough to coat the back of a spoon – don't allow it to boil.
When you draw a finger through the custard on the back of the
spoon, it should leave a clean line.
4. Whisk in the buttermilk, vanilla and salt by hand. Cover the
custard with cling film, pressing it directly onto the surface
to prevent a skin from forming. Cool completely for at least
2 hours, and then freeze in an ice-cream maker according to
the manufacturer's instructions.

Red Velvet Ice Cream

**Makes 950ml (1¾ pints)
ice cream**

For the ice cream
350ml (12fl oz) double
  cream
200g (7oz) caster sugar
1½ tbsp cocoa powder
6 large egg yolks
295ml (10fl oz) buttermilk
1 tsp red gel paste
  colouring
1 tsp vanilla extract

**For the cream cheese
swirl**
115g (4oz) full-fat cream
  cheese, such as
  Philadelphia, cold
40g (1½oz) unsalted butter,
  softened
160g (5½oz) icing sugar
1 tbsp vanilla extract
2 tbsp double cream

*Ice-cream maker and
piping bag fitted with a
large flat-tip nozzle*

We know that our home bakers like to get things perfect, so please don't fret about getting a deep red colour when making Red Velvet ice cream. Layering the ice cream with the cream cheese mixture will produce a homemade-style swirl when you scoop out the finished ice cream after it has set.

1. To make the red velvet ice cream base, in a medium saucepan mix the double cream with 160g (5½oz) of the sugar and the cocoa powder. Heat over a medium-high heat, whisking occasionally, until the sugar and cocoa have dissolved into the cream and the mixture is warm.

2. In another bowl, combine the egg yolks and the remaining sugar, whisking until smooth.

3. Once the cream mixture is warm, slowly pour it into the egg yolks and sugar, whisking constantly to make sure that the eggs don't scramble. Return the egg and cream mixture to the saucepan. Heat over a medium-high heat, stirring constantly and scraping the bottom with a spatula, until it thickens enough to coat the back of a spoon. When you draw a finger through the custard on the back of the spoon, it should leave a clean line.

4. Pour the custard into a bowl and stir in the buttermilk, red food colouring and vanilla. Cover the custard with cling film, pressing it directly onto the surface to prevent a skin forming. Refrigerate for at least 4 hours until completely chilled.

5. To make the cream cheese swirl, mix the cream cheese and butter using a freestanding electric mixer with the paddle attachment or a hand-held electric whisk. Beat on a medium-high speed for about 2 minutes until light and fluffy. Sift in the icing sugar and mix on a low speed just until incorporated. Blend in the vanilla and double cream then increase the speed to medium-high and beat for 2–3 minutes more.

6. Put the cream cheese swirl mix into a piping bag fitted with a large flat-tip nozzle, as this will make it easier to layer the frosting with the ice cream, and put into the refrigerator.

▼

7. To assemble the ice cream, freeze the red velvet ice cream base in an ice-cream maker according to the manufacturer's instructions. Once the base is ready, scoop enough ice cream to cover the bottom of a storage container. Pipe on a generous layer of the cream cheese swirl and scoop some more ice cream to cover, then keep alternating until you've used up all the ice cream and cream cheese swirl.

8. Transfer to the freezer and freeze until firm. The colour might seem pink or salmony while in the ice-cream maker, but it should darken and develop when the ice cream is in the freezer.

Grasshopper Pie Ice Cream

Makes 950ml (1¾ pints) ice cream

350ml (12fl oz) whole milk
2 peppermint tea bags
350ml (12fl oz) double cream
160g (5½oz) caster sugar
4 large egg yolks
1 tsp pure mint extract (optional)
3-5 drops green liquid food colouring (optional)
100g (3½oz) Oreo cookies, broken up
85g (3oz) dark chocolate chips

Ice-cream maker

This mint choc-chip ice cream is livened up and made more like its namesake, Grasshopper Pie, by using Oreo cookies. You can use a mix of white and dark chocolate chips if you like – folding everything in while the ice cream is still soft.

1. In a medium saucepan, heat the milk over a low-medium heat to a gentle simmer, then take off the heat. Add the peppermint tea bags and allow to steep for at least 2 hours until the milk is at room temperature. When ready, wring out the tea bags and discard.
2. Combine the cream, steeped mint milk and sugar in a separate saucepan and bring to a simmer over a medium heat, stirring occasionally. Continue to simmer for about 5 minutes until the sugar dissolves.
3. Using a freestanding electric mixer with the whisk attachment or a hand-held electric whisk, whisk the egg yolks for about 3 minutes until foamy and light in colour.
4. Remove the cream mixture from the heat and slowly pour about half a cup into the egg yolks, whisking constantly so as not to cook the yolks. Pour the cream and egg mixture back into the pan and cook over a medium heat, stirring constantly with a wooden spoon, for about 3–5 minutes until the mixture thickens slightly and coats the back of the spoon. When you draw a finger through the custard on the back of the spoon, it should leave a clean line.
5. If you're satisfied with the mint flavour of the mixture, you won't need the mint extract. However, 1 teaspoon is recommended to give it an added minty lift. Stir in the mint extract and the food colouring, if using.
6. Cover the custard with cling film, pressing it directly onto the surface to prevent a skin from forming. Refrigerate for at least 4 hours until completely chilled.
7. Freeze in an ice-cream maker according to the manufacturer's instructions. Fold the Oreo cookies and chocolate chips into the finished ice cream while it's still in the bowl of the ice-cream maker.

Pumpkin Ice Cream

Makes 950ml (1¾ pints) ice cream

220g (8oz) tinned pumpkin purée
(such as Libby's)
1 tsp vanilla extract
470ml (16½fl oz) double cream
150g (5½oz) soft dark brown sugar
5 large egg yolks
½ tsp ground cinnamon
½ tsp ground ginger
½ tsp ground nutmeg
¼ tsp salt
1 tbsp Kentucky bourbon or whiskey (optional)

Ice-cream maker

The colour of this ice cream is so appealing; you can taste and smell the spices in each bite. You can be a tad more liberal with the whiskey, if you're using it, as it adds a great depth to the flavour. Using brown sugar to make this ice cream gives it a richer taste.

1. To make the ice cream, whisk together the pumpkin purée and vanilla extract. Set aside in the refrigerator while you go through the rest of the steps.

2. In a medium saucepan over a medium heat, combine 350ml (12fl oz) of the cream and 100g (3½oz) of the brown sugar. Simmer gently until the sugar has dissolved.

3. In a bowl, combine the egg yolks, cinnamon, ginger, nutmeg, salt, the remaining cream and the remaining brown sugar. Whisk until smooth and the sugar begins to dissolve.

4. Remove the cream mixture from the heat. Carefully whisk about half a cup of the hot cream mixture into the egg mixture until smooth, being careful to whisk continuously so as not to cook the egg yolks.

5. Pour the egg mixture back into the rest of the cream mixture in the saucepan. Cook over a medium heat, stirring constantly with a wooden spoon and keeping the custard at a low simmer, until it is thick enough to coat the back of the spoon. When you draw a finger through the custard on the back of the spoon, it should leave a clean line. Cool the custard in the fridge for about 1 hour, stirring occasionally.

6. Whisk the pumpkin mixture into the custard. Cover the custard with cling film, pressing it directly onto the surface to prevent a skin from forming. Refrigerate for another hour.

7. Freeze the ice cream in an ice-cream maker according to the manufacturer's instructions. Add the bourbon or whiskey in the last minute or two of churning, if using.

Earl Grey Tea and Chocolate Ice Cream

Makes 950ml (1¾ pints) ice cream

470ml (16½fl oz) double cream
470ml (16½fl oz) whole milk
215g (7½oz) caster sugar
60g (2oz) cocoa powder
½ tsp vanilla extract
2 Earl Grey tea bags
10 large egg yolks
Pinch of salt

Ice-cream maker

If you like Earl Grey tea as much as we do and you know that you're making this ice cream in advance, our hint is to soak the Earl Grey teabags in the milk for a few hours before you start. You can leave out the teabags entirely if you want to make a really good plain chocolate ice cream.

1. Place the cream, milk, half the sugar, the cocoa powder, vanilla extract and Earl Grey tea bags in a large saucepan. Heat slowly for 10–15 minutes, keeping it just under a simmer.
2. Using a freestanding electric mixer with the paddle attachment or a hand-held electric whisk, beat the egg yolks, the remaining half of the sugar and a pinch of salt until the egg yolks have thickened and are slightly lighter in colour.
3. Remove the tea bags from the milk mixture. Whisk half a cup of the hot milk mixture into the egg mixture to warm it up. Then, slowly whisk the egg mixture back into the rest of the milk mixture in the saucepan. Stir the custard over a low heat until thick enough to coat the back of a spoon. When you draw a finger through the custard on the back of the spoon, it should leave a clean line.
4. Take off the heat and cool quickly by placing the pan in a bowl of ice water. Stir occasionally until cooled. Refrigerate until very cold.
5. Freeze in an ice-cream maker according to the manufacturer's instructions.

South Carolina Fig Ice Cream

Makes 480ml (17fl oz) ice cream

15 ripe figs
2 tbsp sherry (optional)
1 tsp vanilla extract
2 large eggs, separated
80g (3oz) caster sugar
235ml (8fl oz) whole milk
235ml (8fl oz) double
   cream

Ice-cream maker

This is an old-fashioned recipe dating from the time when ice cream was made in hand-cranked churners using salt and ice to freeze the custard, so it has a slightly different method from the other recipes in this chapter. Be sure to add the pulped figs only once the ice cream has half frozen in your machine.

1. Scoop out the pulp of the figs and mash well in a bowl. Add the sherry, if using, and the vanilla to the mashed pulp and set aside.
2. Using a freestanding electric mixer with the paddle attachment or a hand-held electric whisk, mix the egg yolks and 40g (1½oz) of the sugar until light and thickened.
3. Heat the milk and cream in a saucepan until hot, but not boiling, and pour over the egg mixture carefully, whisking briskly so as not to cook the yolks. Return the mixture to the saucepan and continue heating until quite hot, but don't boil.
4. While the milk and yolks are heating, briskly whisk the egg whites and the rest of the sugar using a freestanding electric mixer with the whisk attachment or a hand-held electric whisk until they reach the stiff peaks stage. Fold the egg whites into the hot custard and stir. Cover the custard with cling film, pressing it directly onto the surface to prevent a skin from forming, and allow to cool in the fridge for about 2 hours.
5. Start to freeze the custard in an ice-cream maker according to the manufacturer's instructions. When the mixture is half frozen, stir in the fig mixture and continue churning until frozen.

Fresh Peach Ice Cream

**Makes 950ml (1¾ pints)
ice cream**

2 very ripe peaches
215g (7½oz) caster sugar
3½ tbsp Kentucky bourbon
 or whiskey
625ml (1 pint 1fl oz)
 whole milk
315ml (11fl oz) double
 cream
1 tsp vanilla extract
4 large egg yolks

Ice-cream maker

In the USA, Georgia is famous for its peaches and is known as the Peach State. One of the main streets in Atlanta is called Peachtree Street. It's really important that you use very ripe, sweet fresh peaches for this ice cream. Nectarines or similar could be used too, but again, make sure they're sweet and soft.

1. Peel the peaches by scoring the skins with an X using a sharp paring knife. Then plunge them into a bowl of just-boiled water for about 45 seconds. Remove from the hot water and peel off the skin. Cut the peaches roughly into cubes. Mix with 35g (1¼oz) of the caster sugar and the bourbon or whiskey and set aside to macerate.
2. Put the milk, cream and vanilla into a saucepan over a medium heat and bring to a light simmer.
3. While the milk and cream are heating up, use a freestanding electric mixer with the paddle attachment or a hand-held electric whisk to beat the egg yolks and remaining caster sugar until the egg yolks thicken and become lighter in colour.
4. Pour half a cup of the hot milk into the egg yolks to warm them up, whisking constantly, then pour everything back into the rest of the milk mixture in the saucepan and cook for 5–7 minutes until the mixture thickens and coats the back of a spoon, but don't boil. When you draw a finger through the custard on the back of the spoon, it should leave a clean line. Remove from the heat, return the custard to the bowl, then cover with cling film, pressing it directly onto the surface to prevent a skin forming. Put into the fridge for at least 2 hours to cool.
5. Pour the cooled custard into the ice-cream machine and start to freeze. When the ice cream starts to thicken but is still soft, add the peaches and bourbon and continue to freeze according to the manufacturer's instructions.

Peanut Butter Ice Cream

**Makes 950ml (1¾ pints)
ice cream**

350ml (12fl oz) whole milk
350ml (12fl oz) double
  cream
Pinch of salt
6 large egg yolks
150g (5½oz) caster sugar
145g (5oz) smooth peanut
  butter

Ice-cream maker

Most American households have a jar of peanut butter in the store
cupboard, and as well as being spread on bread to make a classic
PB&J sandwich, it can also be used to make delicious things such
as this ice cream. We've decorated our scoops with peanut brittle,
a recipe you can easily find online.

1. Put the milk, double cream and salt into a large saucepan over
a medium heat and bring to a light simmer.
2. Using a freestanding electric mixer with the paddle attachment
or a hand-held electric whisk, beat the egg yolks and sugar until
the egg yolks have thickened and are lighter in colour.
3. Pour half a cup of the hot milk into the yolks and sugar and whisk
briskly to warm up the yolks. Stir the egg mixture back into the rest
of the milk in the saucepan and stir constantly with a wooden spoon
over a medium heat for about 3–5 minutes until you have a thick
custard that coats the back of a spoon. When you draw a finger
through the custard on the back of the spoon, it should leave a
clean line. Mix in the peanut butter, whisking briskly.
4. Take off the heat and cool quickly by placing the pan in a bowl of
ice water. Cover with cling film, pressing it directly onto the surface
to prevent a skin forming, and put it in the fridge for at least 2 hours.
5. Pour the mixture into an ice-cream maker and freeze according
to the manufacturer's instructions.

Lemon Custard Ice Cream

**Makes 950ml (1¾ pints)
ice cream**

215g (7½oz) caster sugar
2 tbsp plain flour
Pinch of salt
470ml (16½fl oz) whole milk
2 large eggs, lightly beaten
235ml (8fl oz) double
    cream
100ml (3½fl oz) evaporated
    milk (unsweetened)
1 tsp vanilla extract
200ml (7fl oz) fresh
    lemon juice

Ice cream maker

Many American recipes use evaporated milk to form a custard-like mixture. Evaporated milk is basically unsweetened condensed milk, so be careful you don't use condensed milk instead, as your results will be way too sweet! We've not put in any lemon extract, as we prefer the more natural taste that fresh lemon juice gives to the ice cream.

1. In a large saucepan, combine the sugar, flour, salt and milk. Whisking briskly, bring to a boil over a medium heat, then cook, stirring continuously, until thickened.
2. Whisk a small amount of the hot milk mixture into the eggs to warm them up, making sure you whisk briskly so that the eggs don't cook. Return everything to the pan, whisking constantly. Continue cooking, without boiling, until the custard thickens enough to coat the back of a spoon. When you draw a finger through the custard on the back of the spoon, it should leave a clean line.
3. Remove from the heat, stir in the cream, evaporated milk, vanilla extract and lemon juice, then cool quickly by placing the pan in a bowl of ice water. Stir for 2 minutes until the mixture has cooled down. Cover the custard with cling film, pressing it directly onto the surface to prevent a skin forming, and put it in the fridge for at least 2 hours.
4. Pour the mixture into your ice-cream maker and freeze according to the manufacturer's instructions.

Puddings

Bourbon Bread Pudding
Bananas Foster Bread Pudding
Praline Bread Pudding with
    Pecan Caramel Sauce
Brownie Pudding
Apple Bread Pudding
White Chocolate Bread Pudding
Hasty Pudding

Bourbon Bread Pudding

**Makes a 23 x 32cm
(9 x 13in) tin, to scoop
or serve as desired**

For the pudding
3 large eggs
215g (7½oz) golden
  caster sugar
950ml (1¾ pints)
  whole milk
1 tsp vanilla extract
½ tsp grated nutmeg
500g (1lb 2oz) stale French
  bread, cut into 2–3cm
  (¾–1¼in) cubes
165g (6oz) raisins

**For the bourbon
whiskey sauce**
295ml (10fl oz) water
100g (3½oz) light
  muscovado sugar
¼ tsp grated nutmeg
1½ tsp cornflour
60ml (2fl oz) Kentucky
  bourbon or whiskey
30g (1oz) unsalted butter

One 23 x 32cm (9 x 13in) tin

In Louisiana, this is known as Creole bread pudding. People in Louisiana who were descended from French, Spanish and African settlers were known as Creoles, and their influence on culture and cooking has made New Orleans unique. If you keep your bread cubes small and press them into the egg mixture, the result will be more pudding-like and less bready.

1. Preheat the oven to 175°C (350°F), Gas mark 4. Grease the tin with butter.
2. Using a freestanding electric mixer with the whisk attachment or a hand-held electric whisk, beat the eggs until frothy. Beat in the sugar, milk, vanilla and nutmeg and mix well.
3. Add the bread and raisins and stir very well by hand until all the bread is as evenly covered as possible. Set aside and leave to soak for 20 minutes.
4. Pour into the prepared tin evenly, pressing down gently on the bread so that the top is as even as possible and the bread is not breaking the surface too much. Bake for 45 minutes.
5. To make the bourbon whiskey sauce, mix the water, brown sugar and nutmeg in a saucepan and bring to the boil on a high heat.
6. In a bowl, mix the cornflour and bourbon together, removing any lumps, then scrape it into the water and sugar mixture and cook until the mixture thickens and is smooth – whisking often. This should take around 8–10 minutes. Remove from the heat and stir in the butter to get a glossy shine on the sauce. Pour the sauce over the bread pudding and serve.

Bananas Foster Bread Pudding

**Makes a 23 x 32cm
(9 x 13in) tin, to scoop
or serve as desired**

450g (1lb) stale French
   bread, cut into 2–3cm
   (¾–1¼in) cubes
700ml (1 pint 4fl oz)
   whipping cream
235ml (8fl oz) whole milk
200g (7oz) caster sugar
100g (3½oz) soft light
   brown sugar
4 large eggs, lightly beaten
3 ripe bananas, mashed
60ml (2fl oz) dark rum
¾ tsp ground cinnamon
2 tsp vanilla extract

For the sauce
170g (6oz) unsalted butter
150g (5½oz) dark
   muscovado sugar
½ tsp ground cinnamon
100ml (3½fl oz) dark rum
80ml (3fl oz) banana
   liqueur (optional)
2 ripe bananas, sliced in
   half lengthways and then
   into half moons

One 23 x 32cm (9 x 13in) tin

This is a dark, rich bread pudding that you slice up and serve with a thick caramelly banana sauce. For added effect, pour a bit of rum on top of each individual serving and flambé at the table!

1. It is best to use stale bread for this, but if your bread is not stale, preheat the oven to 100°C (200°F), Gas mark ¼ and dry out the cubes of bread on a baking sheet for about 10 minutes. Don't let them get toasted; just dry them to simulate stale bread. Remove from the oven then increase the oven temperature to 150°C (300°F), Gas mark 2. Grease the tin with butter, then add the toasted bread cubes, spreading them out evenly.
2. Using a freestanding electric mixer with the paddle attachment or a hand-held electric whisk, mix the cream, milk, sugars, eggs, bananas, rum, cinnamon and vanilla extract together until nice and smooth.
3. Pour the mixture carefully over the cubed bread. Use your fingers to press the bread into the liquid so that the top is as even as possible and the bread is not breaking the surface too much. Leave to soak for 15 minutes in the tin. The bread should start to break down a little as it soaks.
4. Cover the top of the tin with foil and bake for 1½–2 hours. The pudding is ready when a skewer inserted into the centre comes out clean. Remove the foil and bake for another 15–20 minutes, until the top is golden.
5. To make the sauce, melt the butter in a saucepan and add the brown sugar and cinnamon, whisking well. Add the rum to the mixture and ignite with a match – be very careful! Let the flames subside completely, and then stir in the banana liqueur, if using. Add the banana slices and simmer over a medium heat for about 2–3 minutes or until the sauce coats the back of a spoon.
6. Pour the sauce over the bread pudding, cut into squares and serve. Or pour the sauce over individual portions, giving each person some of the cooked sliced banana.

Praline Bread Pudding with Pecan Caramel Sauce

Makes a 23 x 32cm (9 x 13in) tin, to scoop or serve as desired

For the bread pudding
8 large eggs
470ml (16½fl oz) whole milk
470ml (16½fl oz) whipping cream
150g (5½oz) soft light brown sugar
1 tbsp vanilla extract
1 tsp ground cinnamon
1 tsp salt
450g (1lb) challah bread or brioche

For the topping
80g (3oz) unsalted butter, cold and cubed
100g (3½oz) soft dark brown sugar
50g (1¾oz) plain flour
¼ tsp salt
130g (4½oz) chopped pecans

For the sauce
115ml (4fl oz) whole milk
115ml (4fl oz) whipping cream
200g (7oz) soft light brown sugar
115g (4oz) unsalted butter
65g (2oz) chopped pecans
½ tsp vanilla extract
1 tbsp Kentucky bourbon or whiskey

One 23 x 32cm (9 x 13in) tin

Pralines and bread pudding are a New Orleans treat, so putting them together is a natural next step! Using a sweet brioche gives it a Creole twist. A lot of ingredients go into this, but the rich result will go far.

1. Preheat the oven to 175°C (350°F), Gas mark 4. Grease the tin with butter.
2. To make the bread pudding, using a freestanding electric mixer with the paddle attachment or a hand-held electric whisk, mix the eggs, milk, cream, brown sugar, vanilla, cinnamon and salt together until smooth.
3. Cut the bread into 2cm (¾in) cubes and add to the egg mixture, carefully stirring and pressing the bread in so that it evenly absorbs the liquid. Set aside for 20 minutes at room temperature.
4. To make the topping, in a large bowl and with cold fingertips, gently rub the butter into the brown sugar, flour and salt until crumbly. Fold in the pecans so that they're all evenly mixed.
5. Transfer the soaked bread into the prepared tin, pressing down gently on the bread so that the top is as even as possible and the bread is not breaking the surface too much. Evenly sprinkle the topping over the top of the soggy bread. Bake for 40–45 minutes.
6. To make the sauce, mix the milk, cream, brown sugar and butter together in a small saucepan and bring to a boil over a medium-high heat, stirring occasionally. Boil for 4 minutes. Stir in the pecans, vanilla, bourbon and a pinch of salt and continue to boil for 2 more minutes. Remove the pan from the heat and allow the sauce to cool to room temperature. Either pour the sauce over the whole pudding or over individual servings.

Brownie Pudding

**Makes a 23 x 32cm
(9 x 13in) tin, to scoop
or serve as desired**

For the pudding
245g (8½oz) plain flour
3½ tsp baking powder
¾ tsp salt
295g (10½oz) caster sugar
30g (1oz) cocoa powder
250ml (9fl oz) evaporated
    milk (unsweetened)
2 tsp vanilla extract
50g (1¾oz) butter, melted
200g (7oz) chopped
    pecans

For the topping
275g (10oz) soft light brown
    sugar
60g (2oz) cocoa powder
750ml (1 pint 6fl oz) hot
    water (boil then let cool
    slightly)

One 23 x 32cm (9 x 13in) tin

This baked pudding ends up with a soft brownie-like texture and is incredibly easy to make, as it doesn't really require much in terms of assembly and mixing. Once it's ready, the top will be firm to the touch, but the middle will still be soft and gooey, so the skewer test shouldn't be used here.

1. Preheat the oven to 175°C (350°F), Gas mark 4. Grease the tin with butter.
2. To make the pudding, whisk together the flour, baking powder, salt, sugar and cocoa in a bowl.
3. Using a freestanding electric mixer with the paddle attachment or a hand-held electric whisk, beat the evaporated milk, vanilla and melted butter into the dry ingredients until smooth. Fold in the pecans by hand and spread the mixture evenly in the tin.
4. To make the topping, mix the brown sugar and cocoa together and sprinkle over the mixture in the tin. Pour the hot water over the entire pudding.
5. Bake for 40–45 minutes, until the top is firm to touch. Leave to stand for 5 minutes before serving.

Apple Bread Pudding

Makes a 23 x 32cm (9 x 13in) tin, to scoop or serve as desired

For the brandy or whiskey custard

235ml (8fl oz) double cream
2 large egg yolks
55g (2oz) caster sugar
1 cinnamon stick
2 tbsp apple brandy such as Calvados, or Kentucky bourbon or whiskey

For the pudding

30g (1oz) unsalted butter
3 large apples (such as Pink Lady), peeled, cored and cut into 5mm–1cm (¼–½in) cubes
700ml (1 pint 4fl oz) double cream
4 large eggs
1 large egg yolk
55g (2oz) caster sugar
1 tsp ground cinnamon
455g (1lb) stale Cinnamon Raisin Swirl loaf (see page 238), pain au raisin or other cinnamon bread, cut into 2–3cm (¾–1¼in) cubes
4 tbsp demerara sugar

One 23 x 32cm (9 x 13in) tin

In the USA, cinnamon swirl bread is easy to buy, and makes this bread pudding extra special. We show you how to make it on page 238, but you can also use any sort of cinnamon bread that you can find.

1. To make the custard, whisk the cream, egg yolks, sugar and cinnamon together in a saucepan and cook over a medium heat for 8–10 minutes. Don't let it boil, and whisk constantly. The custard should thicken enough to coat the back of a spoon.
2. Pass through a fine sieve to remove any lumps but retain the cinnamon stick. Stir in the Calvados, bourbon or whiskey. Cover the top of the custard with cling film, pressing it directly onto the surface. Put into the fridge for at least 2 hours, stirring very often. Chill until the custard is cool and set. Remove the cinnamon stick.
3. To make the pudding, preheat the oven to 190°C (375°F), Gas mark 5. Grease the tin with butter.
4. Melt the butter in a frying pan over a medium heat and cook the apples for 8–10 minutes until lightly browned. Stir occasionally.
5. In the bowl of a freestanding electric mixer with the paddle attachment or using a hand-held electric whisk, whisk the cream, eggs, egg yolk, caster sugar and cinnamon together until smooth. Stir in the bread cubes by hand and allow to soak for 20 minutes, pressing the bread into the liquid. Carefully stir in the cooked apples.
6. Sprinkle half the demerara sugar onto the base of the greased tin and spoon in the soaked bread and liquid, pressing down gently on the bread so the top is as even as possible and the bread is not breaking the surface too much. Sprinkle with the rest of the demerara sugar.
7. Bake for 40–45 minutes until the pudding is light golden and set. Serve with the brandy or whiskey custard.

White Chocolate Bread Pudding

**Makes a 23 x 32cm
(9 x 13in) tin, to scoop
or serve as desired**

250g (9oz) French bread,
   cut into 2–3cm
   (¾–1¼in) cubes
800ml (1 pint 9fl oz)
   whipping cream
235ml (8fl oz) whole milk
100g (3½oz) caster sugar
500g (1lb 2oz) white
   chocolate, chopped
5 large egg yolks
2 large eggs
1 tbsp dark rum

*One 23 x 32cm (9 x 13in) tin
or 2-litre (3½-pint) pudding
dish*

We wanted to recreate the fabulous bread pudding served at the famous Palace Café on Canal Street in New Orleans. Bread puddings abound in New Orleans and this white chocolate version is something special. If your bread is stale, so much the better!

1. Preheat the oven to 135°C (275°F), Gas mark 1.
2. Place the bread cubes evenly on a baking sheet and bake for about 20 minutes until light golden and dry. Remove the bread from the oven and let it cool. Increase the oven temperature to 175°C (350°F), Gas mark 4 while you prepare the rest of the pudding.
3. Mix 700ml (1 pint 4fl oz) of the whipping cream, all the milk and the sugar in a saucepan and bring to a simmer over a medium heat, stirring until the sugar dissolves. Remove from the heat, add 285g (10oz) of the white chocolate and stir until melted and smooth. Whisk the yolks and whole eggs together in a large bowl and gradually add the warm chocolate and milk mixture.
4. Place the bread cubes into the tin or pudding dish and pour on half the chocolate mixture. Mix and press the bread cubes into the chocolate mixture so that everything is evenly covered and allow to soak in for 15 minutes.
5. Gently mix the remaining chocolate mixture into the soaked bread cubes, being careful not to break up the cubes. Cover the dish with foil and bake the pudding for 40 minutes. Take off the foil and bake for about 15 minutes more until the top is golden brown. Remove from the oven and allow to cool slightly.
6. To make the white chocolate sauce, simmer the remaining 100ml (3½fl oz) cream with the rum over a low-medium heat. Remove the saucepan from the heat, add the remaining white chocolate and stir until melted and smooth. Pour the sauce over the pudding and serve.

Hasty Pudding

**Makes a 23 x 32cm
(9 x 13in) tin, to scoop
or serve as desired**

1.4 litres (2 pints 6fl oz)
   whole milk
115g (4oz) unsalted butter
85g (3oz) yellow cornmeal
   (polenta)
35g (1¼oz) plain flour
1 tsp salt
120g (4oz) pure cane
   molasses, such
   as Meridian
3 large eggs
70g (2½oz) caster sugar
1 tsp ground cinnamon
1 tsp ground nutmeg
165g (6oz) raisins

One 23 x 32cm (9 x 13in) tin

New Englanders have been making and eating Hasty Pudding
(also known as Indian Pudding) since the early settlers arrived in
the 1620s. The Native Americans they encountered taught them
how to use cornmeal in their cooking, as wheat flour was scarce.

1. Preheat the oven to 120°C (250°F), Gas mark ½.
2. Heat the milk and butter in a heatproof bowl set over, but not
touching, a pan of gently boiling water. The milk should be very hot
and small bubbles should begin to appear around the edge – but
it should not boil. Transfer the milk and butter to a saucepan and
keep warm on the hob on a low-medium heat.
3. In a separate bowl, mix together the cornmeal, flour and salt and
stir in the molasses. Mix about half a cup of the scalded milk into the
cornmeal mixture, a few tablespoons at a time, then gradually add
the mixture back into the large pan of milk. Cook, stirring often, for
about 5 minutes until thickened.
4. Beat the eggs in a bowl, then warm them by slowly adding a half
cup of the hot milk and cornmeal mixture, whisking constantly and
making sure you do not scramble the eggs. Add the egg mixture to
the remaining hot milk and cornmeal mixture and stir to combine.
Stir in the sugar and spices until smooth.
5. The mixture should be smooth – you can strain it through
a sieve (not a fine one) or put it into a food processor to achieve
this. Stir in the raisins by hand and pour into the tin.
6. Bake for 2 hours. Remove from the oven and allow the pudding
to cool for about an hour. Serve warm.

Bread & Savouries

Buttermilk Biscuits
Sally Lunn Loaf
Skillet Cornbread
Sweet Potato Cornbread
Crawfish Pie
Pumpkin Crumb Muffins
Cinnamon Raisin Swirl Loaf
Sweet Potato Biscuits
New Orleans Beignets
Graham Crackers

Buttermilk Biscuits

Makes 12 biscuits

300g (10½oz) plain flour
½ tsp bicarbonate of soda
75g (2½oz) cold unsalted
   butter, cut into small
   cubes
235ml (8fl oz) buttermilk

5cm (2in) circular cutter

Biscuits made with buttermilk are a Southern staple and, despite the name, bear no similarity to British biscuits. Instead, they are pillowy and light, a softer scone, and are served with bacon, eggs and grits for breakfast, or even with fried chicken and gravy for dinner. They are definitely best eaten on the day they're made.

1. Preheat the oven to 200°C (400°F), Gas mark 6. Line a baking sheet with non-stick baking parchment.
2. Sift the flour and bicarbonate of soda together into a cold bowl. With very cold, dry fingers, rub the butter into the flour until evenly mixed. Pour in the buttermilk and, by hand, gently mix together until a dough is formed.
3. On a lightly floured surface, roll out the dough to about a 1cm (½in) thickness, then cut into rounds with a 5cm (2in) circular cutter.
4. Place the biscuits on the prepared baking sheet and bake for 10–12 minutes until golden brown. Cool briefly on the sheet and then transfer to a wire rack to cool completely.

Sally Lunn Loaf

Makes one 25cm (10in) ring cake, to slice as desired

235ml (8fl oz) lukewarm
  milk
1 tsp caster sugar
1 tbsp dried active yeast
540g (1lb 3oz) plain flour
95g (3½oz) caster sugar
1 tsp salt
3 large eggs, lightly beaten
½ tsp bicarbonate of soda
120ml (4fl oz) warm water
110g (4oz) unsalted butter,
  melted

*One 25cm (10in) tube pan
or ring mould*

The name Sally Lunn comes from a type of bun made in Bath, first recorded in the eighteenth century. It was then brought over to the USA and changed a little, and now this sweet bread made with yeast and bicarbonate of soda forms the perfect base for frying up a weekend French toast breakfast treat.

1. Grease the tube pan or ring mould liberally with butter.
2. Stir the milk, sugar and yeast together in a large jug and leave to stand for 5 minutes.
3. Whisk the flour, caster sugar and salt together in a large bowl and stir in the eggs, bicarbonate of soda and warm water until well blended. Add the yeast mixture and the melted butter and stir until well incorporated.
4. Scrape the batter into the prepared tube pan or ring mould and cover with cling film. Let the doughy batter rise in a warm place, such as an airing cupboard or near a radiator, for 45 minutes–1 hour until it has doubled in size.
5. Preheat the oven to 200°C (400°F), Gas mark 6.
6. Carefully put the pan into the oven, making sure not to move the dough about too much or knock the air bubbles out of it. Bake for 25–30 minutes, until a skewer inserted into the centre comes out clean. Remove from the oven and allow to cool on a wire rack for 30 minutes before serving.

Skillet Cornbread

Makes one 25cm (10in) cornbread, to slice as desired

340g (12oz) yellow cornmeal (polenta)
35g (1¼oz) plain flour
2 tsp baking powder
2 tsp bicarbonate of soda
2 tsp salt
2 tbsp caster sugar
2 large eggs, lightly beaten
470ml (16½fl oz) buttermilk
3 tbsp vegetable oil, dripping or lard

One 25cm (10in) cast-iron skillet or ovenproof pan

This traditional cornbread recipe would most definitely have been made with lard melted in a very hot skillet, poured into the batter and then the batter poured back to sizzle in the skillet and bake in the oven. Cornbread is served with meals as you would normal bread, and is amazing when eaten warm with a lot of butter!

1. Preheat the oven to 200°C (400°F), Gas mark 6.
2. Sift the cornmeal, flour, baking powder, bicarbonate of soda, salt and sugar into a large bowl (make sure this is not plastic as you'll be pouring hot oil into it). Mix the eggs and buttermilk together in a bowl, then add to the dry ingredients and mix to combine.
3. On the hob, heat the oil, dripping or lard in your skillet or pan until smoking lightly. Swirl the hot fat around the pan to coat it, then carefully pour the hot fat into the batter and stir until it's well blended in.
4. Pour the batter into the very hot pan – it should sizzle. Bake in the oven for about 20 25 minutes until the top is golden and the cornbread pulls away from the sides. Serve hot.

Sweet Potato Cornbread

Makes a 900g (2lb) loaf

1 large or 1½ medium sweet
  potatoes
170g (6oz) yellow cornmeal
  (polenta)
55g (2oz) caster sugar
135g (5oz) plain flour
½ tsp bicarbonate of soda
1½ tsp baking powder
¼ tsp salt
2 large eggs
175g (6oz) full-fat soured
  cream
1 tsp vanilla extract
55g (2oz) unsalted butter,
  melted

One 900g (2lb) loaf tin

A tasty variant of cornbread that uses sweet potatoes to give flavour
and colour, this can be served alongside a meal in place of regular
bread. You can also toast the slices and spread them with butter
and jam, or even use the bread as the base for some of the recipes
in the Pudding chapter.

1. Preheat the oven to 200°C (400°F), Gas mark 6. Grease
the loaf tin with butter or line with non-stick baking parchment.
2. Wrap the sweet potatoes in foil and bake for about
45–60 minutes until tender. Once cooled, scoop out the flesh and
mash in a bowl. Push through a sieve to make a really smooth purée.
Set aside. Lower the oven temperature to 190°C (375°F), Gas mark 5.
3. Put the cornmeal and sugar in a bowl. Sift in the flour, bicarbonate
of soda, baking powder and salt. Stir to ensure all the ingredients are
evenly combined.
4. Beat the eggs lightly in a bowl, then add the soured cream, vanilla
and melted butter and whisk until creamy and thick. Stir in the
mashed sweet potatoes and mix well.
5. Add the wet ingredients to the dry ingredients and mix together
gently by hand until thoroughly combined – be careful not to
overmix. Scrape and pour the mixture into the prepared loaf tin
and smooth the top.
6. Bake for 55–65 minutes or until the top is golden brown and
a skewer inserted into the cornbread comes out clean.

Crawfish Pie

**Makes a 23cm (9in) pie,
to slice as desired**

1 x quantity Basic American
Flaky Pastry (see page 92)
or 500g (1lb 2oz) block
shortcrust pastry or
375g (13oz) ready-rolled
shortcrust pastry

For the filling
60g (2oz) unsalted butter
150g (5½oz) white or yellow
onions, chopped
1 green pepper, deseeded
and chopped
1 celery stalk, chopped
1½ tsp salt
½ tsp cayenne pepper
120g (4oz) chopped tinned
tomatoes
450g (1lb) peeled crawfish
(crayfish) tails
2 tbsp cornflour
115ml (4fl oz) water
1 spring onion, chopped
25g (1oz) fresh parsley,
chopped

*One 23cm (9in) pie dish
or foil pie dish*

This is a Cajun and Creole dish from Louisiana, made famous by a
song. We strongly suggest you seek out crayfish tails to get the most
out of this savoury pie, but you could also use shrimps or prawns as
a substitute. You can double up the pastry and put on a top crust
as well if you wish.

1. Preheat the oven to 190°C (375°F), Gas mark 5.
2. To make the pastry, follow the Basic American Flaky Pastry recipe
on page 92. If using shop-bought pastry, roll it out on a lightly
floured surface until it is about 5mm (¼in) thick. Line the pie dish
with the pastry and place in the fridge while you make the filling.
3. Melt the butter in a large pan, then add the onion, pepper
and celery and cook for about 8 minutes until soft and golden.
Add the salt, cayenne pepper and tomatoes and cook for
5 minutes, stirring occasionally. Add the crawfish tails and cook
for 5 more minutes – they should start to give off some liquid.
4. In a bowl, dissolve the cornflour in the water and add it to the
pan. Stir for 2–3 minutes over a medium heat until the mixture
thickens a lot, almost to a paste. Add the spring onion and parsley.
Remove from the heat and allow to cool slightly.
5. Pour the cooked mixture into the pie dish and bake for 45 minutes
to an hour until the edge of the crust is golden. Let it cool for about
10 minutes before serving.

Pumpkin Crumb Muffins

Makes 12 muffins

For the muffins
85g (3oz) unsalted butter, softened
115g (4oz) full-fat cream cheese, such as Philadelphia, softened
110g (4oz) caster sugar
100g (3½oz) light brown sugar
1 large egg
200g (7oz) plain flour
¼ tsp ground cinnamon
¼ tsp ground ginger
Pinch of ground cloves
Pinch of ground nutmeg
¼ tsp baking powder
¼ tsp bicarbonate of soda
¼ tsp salt
165g (6oz) tinned pumpkin purée (such as Libby's)
30g (1oz) pecan nuts, roughly chopped (optional)
¼ tsp vanilla extract

For the crumb topping
30g (1oz) pecan nuts, roughly chopped
50g (1¾oz) light brown sugar
½ tbsp plain flour
⅛ tsp ground cinnamon
⅛ tsp ground ginger
Pinch of ground cloves
10g (⅓oz) unsalted butter, melted

One 12-hole deep muffin tin and 12 paper muffin cases

We wanted to include this muffin recipe in the book because it has a very tasty crumb topping, also known as a streusel topping in the USA. Try not to overfill your paper cases – they should be three-quarters full at most – as you don't want them to rise too much and get the topping over your muffin tray instead of in your mouth!

1. Preheat the oven to 175°C (350°F), Gas mark 4 and line the muffin tin with the paper muffin cases.
2. First, make the crumb topping. Stir the pecans, sugar, flour, spices and melted butter together and set aside.
3. Using a freestanding electric mixer with the paddle attachment or a hand-held electric whisk, beat the butter and cream cheese together until light and creamy. Add both the sugars and beat until fluffy. Don't overbeat or the cream cheese will split. Add the egg, only beating until just incorporated. Scrape down the sides of the bowl.
4. Sift the flour, spices, baking powder, bicarbonate of soda and salt together and add to the butter mixture on a low speed. Mix well, then add the puréed pumpkin, chopped pecan nuts, if using, and vanilla extract. Scoop the mixture into the muffin cases, so that they are three-quarters full. Sprinkle with the crumb topping.
5. Bake for about 25 minutes. When ready, an inserted skewer should come out clean. Cool in the tin for 5 minutes before transferring to a wire rack to cool completely.

Cinnamon Raisin Swirl Loaf

Makes a 900g (2lb) loaf

For the loaf
85g (3oz) unsalted butter
235ml (8fl oz) whole milk
2½ tsp dried active yeast
475g plain flour
1 tsp salt
70g (2½oz) caster sugar
2 large eggs
150g (5½oz) raisins

For the swirl
30g (1oz) butter, melted
70g (2½oz) caster sugar
2 tbsp ground cinnamon

Flavourless vegetable oil,
   rapeseed or corn
1 egg and a splash of milk,
   whisked together for
   brushing

One 900g (2lb) loaf tin

This is a fun loaf to make and is perfect for the base of the Apple Bread Pudding on page 221. Otherwise, serve it at breakfast, slightly toasted with some butter.

1. To make the bread, put the butter and milk in a small saucepan and heat until the butter is melted and bubbles appear around the edge. Do not boil. Allow to cool until still warm to the touch, but not hot. Sprinkle the yeast over the top, stir gently, and allow to sit for 10 minutes.
2. Sift together the flour and salt.
3. Using a freestanding electric mixer with the paddle attachment or a hand-held electric whisk, mix the sugar and eggs until just incorporated. Pour in the milk and yeast mixture and stir to combine. Add half the flour and beat on medium speed until combined. Add the rest of the flour and the raisins and beat until combined.
4. Change to the dough hook attachment and knead the dough on medium speed for 10 minutes. If the dough is overly sticky, add an extra 30g (1oz) flour and beat again for 5 minutes. The dough should be soft.
5. Grease a large mixing bowl with a little flavourless vegetable oil. Place the dough in the bowl and cover with cling film. Set it in a warm, dry place for at least 2 hours, until doubled in size.
6. Turn the dough out onto a lightly floured work surface. It will still be soft. Roll into a neat rectangle, no wider than the widest part of the loaf tin you're going to use, and about 45-60cm (18-24in) long. Brush the top of the rectangle with the melted butter. Mix the sugar and cinnamon together, then sprinkle evenly over the butter-smeared dough.
7. Starting at the far end, roll the dough towards you, keeping it tight and contained. When you finish rolling, pinch the end of the roll onto the main body of the loaf to seal it. Grease the loaf tin with softened butter. Place the dough, seam down, in the tin. Cover with cling film and allow to rise for 2 hours.
8. Towards the end of the 2 hours, preheat the oven to 175°C (350°F), Gas mark 4. Take the cling film off the dough and brush the top with the milk and egg mixture. Bake for 40 minutes, until risen, golden and hollow-sounding when the base is tapped. Remove from the tin and leave to cool completely on a wire rack before slicing.

Sweet Potato Biscuits

Makes about 12–15 biscuits

2–3 sweet potatoes
80ml (3fl oz) buttermilk
270g (9½oz) plain flour
1 tbsp baking powder
40g (1½oz) caster sugar
½ tsp ground cinnamon
¼ tsp ground nutmeg
¼ tsp ground ginger
⅛ tsp ground cloves
½ tsp salt
75g (2½oz) unsalted butter, cold and cut into small cubes

For the marshmallow variation
36–48 mini marshmallows

5cm (2in) round biscuit cutter

These are another type of buttermilk biscuit, with sweet potatoes and spices adding more layers to the flavour. We have included a variation with a marshmallow centre – if you try this out, the biscuits should be served warm.

1. Preheat the oven to 200°C (400°F), Gas mark 6. Line a medium baking sheet with non-stick baking parchment.
2. Wrap the sweet potatoes in foil and bake for about 45–60 minutes until tender. Once cooled, scoop out the flesh and mash in a bowl. Push through a sieve to make a really smooth purée. Set aside to cool. Mix the cooled mashed sweet potatoes with the buttermilk until well blended.
3. Sift the flour, baking powder, sugar, spices and salt into a bowl. With very cold fingers, rub the butter into the flour mixture until it resembles coarse breadcrumbs. Be careful not to overwork the mixture and keep everything cool. Add the blended sweet potato and buttermilk to the flour mixture and use your hands to bring it all together to make a soft dough. Handle as little as possible so as not to overwork it. Allow the dough to cool in the fridge for 15–20 minutes.
4. On a floured surface, lightly roll out the dough or press it out with your fingers to about 2.5cm (1in) thick. Press a 5cm (2in) cutter straight down to cut out the biscuits, making sure not to twist it. Place them on the prepared baking sheet. Bake for 15–20 minutes, until lightly browned.

Variation
To make the marshmallow variation, follow the steps above until you have a chilled dough at the end of step 3.
1. Divide the dough in half. On a floured surface, roll out each half into a similar shape until 1cm (½in) thick. Use the cutter to cut out an even number of circles, pressing the cutter straight down and making sure not to twist it.
2. Sprinkle the marshmallows on top of half the biscuits (about 6 per biscuit). Place a biscuit with no marshmallows on top of each of the marshmallow-topped ones. Use your rolling pin to press the two layers together gently. Bake for 15–20 minutes, until lightly browned.

New Orleans Beignets

**Makes about
40–45 beignets**

235ml (8fl oz) water
235ml (8fl oz) whole milk
1 large egg
400g (14oz) plain flour
2 tbsp baking powder
1 tsp salt
2 tsp sugar
Pinch of ground nutmeg
About 1 litre (1¾ pints)
  vegetable oil, for frying
Icing sugar, for dusting

Our beignets are not as perfectly even as the ones you'd eat at the Café du Monde on Decatur Street in New Orleans. But they've been making beignets and serving them with cups of café au lait, milky coffee blended with chicory, since 1862. Be sure to dust your beignets liberally with icing sugar and eat them while they're warm and fresh.

1. Using a freestanding electric mixer with the whisk attachment or a hand-held electric whisk, combine the water, milk and egg and whisk well. Add the flour, baking powder, salt, sugar and nutmeg and mix until the batter is smooth.
2. Heat the oil in a deep pan or deep-fat fryer to 180°C (355°F). Test with a thermometer or drop in a crouton-sized piece of bread – if it turns golden immediately then the oil is hot enough.
3. Drop the batter a tablespoon at a time into the oil in small batches. Fry for 3–4 minutes until golden brown, making sure to turn the beignets over two or three times to brown them all over. Remove with a slotted spoon, drain on kitchen roll and, once cool, dust with icing sugar. Repeat until you've used all the batter.

Graham Crackers

Makes 48 crackers

200g (7oz) plain flour
120g (4oz) wholemeal flour
55g (2oz) wheatgerm
½ tsp salt
1 tsp bicarbonate of soda
1 tsp ground cinnamon
225g (8oz) unsalted butter,
softened
150g (5½oz) soft light
brown sugar
2 tbsp runny honey

Fluted pastry wheel
(or regular knife)

We're sure all you American baking aficionados out there have seen Graham Crackers listed as an ingredient in many cheesecake and pie recipes. They're not easy to find in the UK, so here's a good recipe for making your own.

1. Preheat the oven to 175°C (350°F), Gas mark 4. Line three large baking sheets with baking parchment.
2. Whisk together the flours, wheatgerm, salt, bicarbonate of soda and cinnamon and set aside.
3. Using a freestanding electric mixer with the paddle attachment or a hand-held electric whisk, cream the butter, sugar and honey together for around 5 minutes on a medium-high speed until light and fluffy. On a lower speed, add the flour mixture and mix until combined.
4. Turn the dough out onto a floured surface and divide into quarters. It is a sticky dough, so roll out each piece between two sheets of non-stick baking parchment to roughly 25 x 16cm (10 x 6in) rectangles, about 3–4mm (⅛in) thick.
5. Using a fluted pastry wheel (or a regular knife), trim the outermost edges of each rectangle and divide into three 8 x 16cm (3 x 6in) rectangles. Then, cut again, but this time press the pastry wheel lightly along the cut, so that you don't cut all the way through, scoring each piece in half lengthways and crossways so that four smaller 4 x 8cm (1½ x 3in) crackers are formed out of each rectangle.
6. Repeat with the rest of the dough. Stack the layers between cling film or baking parchment and put in the freezer to firm up for 10 minutes.
7. Remove two sheets of dough from the freezer. Prick holes in the top of the crackers using the prongs of a fork, making four rows of vertical fork pricks on each small cracker.
8. Transfer to the prepared baking sheets and bake for 8–9 minutes until dark golden brown. You may have to rotate the crackers halfway through baking to get an even colour. When you remove each batch, cut with a knife or pastry wheel while still warm and neaten the edges, so that, once cool, they will separate into individual crackers. Let cool on the baking sheets for 5 minutes, then transfer the crackers to wire racks to cool completely. Repeat with the remaining sheets of dough.

Baking Essentials

You'll find lots of useful advice here, including replies to questions that we are frequently asked and other helpful information from our website, hummingbirdbakery.com (you can also look on the FAQs section of our website, where there is more helpful advice). Using this chapter for reference and following the recipes carefully will help ensure your cakes, pies and cookies turn out perfectly each time. Above all, we hope you have fun making the recipes.

Ingredients

Quality is key when choosing ingredients for baking. For the best results, buy the best you can afford, and always use full-fat dairy products, as the higher fat content is very important for achieving the right texture and flavour. Here is some important information on selected ingredients.

Butter

This should always be unsalted, as salt can affect the taste of the finished dish. If you're using it for making a sponge, it needs to be very soft, so take it out of the fridge an hour or so before you start cooking — or soften it for a few seconds in the microwave if you're pushed for time. For pastry, butter is best straight from the fridge as everything needs to be kept ice cold.

Buttermilk

Like standard cow's milk, this needs to be full fat in order to work properly. It's available from the dairy aisle of most large supermarkets, although you could try substituting with a mixture of half whole milk and half full-fat natural yoghurt.

Cream cheese

Unlike the butter in our frostings which should be at room temperature, cream cheese should always be used cold from the fridge or it will make the frosting runny. Overbeating cream cheese in a recipe will also tend to make a frosting or filling runny and unsalvageable. We only recommend using full-fat Philadelphia cream cheese. Fat content is crucial in helping the recipe to turn out correctly and provides a luxurious and creamy taste.

Cocoa powder and chocolate

Use a really good-quality brand of cocoa powder and good-quality chocolate with a minimum of 70% cocoa solids if you're using dark chocolate. We recommend Green & Black's, but Swiss and Belgian dark or milk chocolate works well so long as you stick to the 70% rule for dark.

Baking powder and bicarbonate of soda

These may only be used in very small quantities, but they are essential for helping a sponge to rise and to prevent it being dense and heavy. They are not interchangeable — each works in a slightly different way to create a reaction. Follow the recipe carefully for the right amount, using level spoon measurements. And do check that they don't linger in your cupboard too long or beyond their 'best before' dates or they may not be so effective.

Vanilla extract

For the best results, it's important to use natural vanilla extract (or 'essence', which means the same thing) rather than an artificial vanilla flavouring.

By all means experiment using vanilla pods, if you prefer, but you may need to make a few batches to get the flavour right.

Food colouring

Liquid food colouring is readily available from any supermarket, but as there are many different brands, all with slightly different colour ranges, you may need to shop around to find your preferred shade. A better colour can usually be obtained from a gel paste, available from cookshops and specialist cake shops or online. You will need less paste than you would liquid; just add a little at a time until you achieve the desired result. A proper deep red is the trickiest colour to achieve. For this a 'non-natural' red gel paste is best — we recommend the Sugarflair or Wilton brands, available online. ('Natural' colourings aren't strong enough to create a good depth of colour and, when baked, your sponges will turn brown rather than red. Adding more will just spoil the flavour and cause the batter or frosting to split.)

Pumpkin

In this book, all the pumpkin we've used is tinned. Libby's brand tinned pumpkin can be found in larger supermarkets in the UK and can be ordered online if you can't find it locally. Although you can bake and mash your own fresh pumpkin purée, it tends to be more watery and less intense than tinned. If you boil fresh pumpkin, it will definitely be too watery when mashed.

Molasses

In the USA molasses is found in every supermarket. It's similar to black treacle, but slightly less dark and less intense. You shouldn't substitute pure treacle for molasses, as it will be too strong. You could mix half black treacle with half golden syrup to approximate American molasses. Here in the UK, you can generally find molasses in health

food shops. Meridian brand Natural Pure Cane molasses is recommended and this can also be bought online.

Bourbon

We've included bourbon in many of the recipes, which is an American whiskey, usually from Kentucky. If you're striving for 100 per cent authenticity, then Jim Bean, Wild Turkey or Maker's Mark are all famous brands of Kentucky bourbon. A Tennessee whiskey, such as Jack Daniels, would be just as good as would any whiskey from the UK.

Gluten- and dairy-free substitutes

At Hummingbird we haven't yet found any good substitutes for dairy products or eggs, although do feel free to experiment yourself to see if you can create something to your taste using dairy-free ingredients. You can use gluten-free flour, however, and we'd recommend the Doves Farm range. You can also substitute bicarbonate of soda and baking powder with gluten-free alternatives.

While most of the ingredients in this book can be bought from a supermarket, you may come across one or two slightly unusual or specialist items. You should find most of these in larger supermarkets or specialist cake stores, but if you don't, then online suppliers who deliver to your door are often the best alternative.

Equipment

Weighing scales

Measuring with accuracy is really important in baking, as the chemical interactions of all the various ingredients are what make your finished sponge or loaf. Digital scales are ideal, therefore, as they give more accurate readings than mechanical ones.

Electric mixers and whisks

Making a cake by hand using only a spoon or whisk is very hard, requiring a great deal of time and effort, which is why most of our recipes call for either a freestanding electric mixer (with a paddle attachment, or 'flat beater' as it's sometimes called) or a hand-held electric whisk. Creaming butter and sugar together for a sponge or whipping a frosting to perfection requires a good few minutes of constant beating, which is almost impossible to achieve by hand. In the USA, before electric whisks and mixers were invented, most frostings were of the boiled variety, which took a lot of stirring but didn't need to be as finely and airily whipped. Unless you're a very keen baker, there's no need to invest in an expensive mixer, however. Hand-held electric whisks (or hand-held blenders with a whisk attachment) can be bought cheaply from larger supermarkets and are useful for all types of cooking, not just baking.

Baking tins

Hummingbird recipes are written with specific tin dimensions in mind, so always use the size of cake tin specified or the cooking time will be affected. Whatever the size of the tin, we recommend you fill it to around two-thirds full. This allows space for the sponge to expand and should help to prevent the mixture from overflowing. Cake tins should be about 5cm (2in) deep.

Sugar thermometer

For making caramels or the various sweet treats in this book, a sugar thermometer is very useful, indeed indispensable if you're a beginner baker, for checking that the mixture has reached the right temperature.

Piping bag

A piping bag is recommended in a number of recipes in this book. A disposable bag — or baking parchment rolled into a cone and taped together — with a hole cut at the tip to the size specified by the recipe can be just as effective as a standard type of bag with a nozzle.

Oven

All the recipes in this book have been tested in a conventional oven. If you are using a fan-assisted oven (which tends to cook things faster), it's a good idea to read the manufacturer's instruction booklet, which will probably recommend turning down the temperature a little. If you no longer have the oven instructions, we suggest reducing the temperature by 10 per cent.

Ice-cream makers

An ice-cream maker is important if you're looking to produce fluffy balls of ice cream free from ice crystals. You can, of course, freeze your mixture in a plastic container in the freezer, making sure you mix thoroughly every hour or so in order to get the ice cream airy and minimise ice crystals, but it is more time-consuming and harder to get a perfect result. There are two types of electric ice cream makers: those that have a bowl that must be frozen in advance, and those that freeze the ice cream whilst churning. The fully automated ice cream machines are a lot more expensive, so do think about your budget and how often you may make ice cream before you purchase.

Methods & Techniques

Sponge Making

When you're baking a Hummingbird cake, you need to follow the recipe exactly as written. Baking isn't a time for experimenting with different proportions; the wrong balance of ingredients can cause a recipe to fail. Our methods may seem unconventional at times, and our proportions not as you're used to, but they are tried and tested, so trust us! See also the following tips:

Sifting dry ingredients

It's good practice to sift flour, cocoa powder and icing sugar before use. This removes lumps and improves the texture of the finished cake.

If combining dry ingredients like these, it is easiest to simply sift them together, then mix them by hand with a spoon. (Avoid mixing them with a machine as this raises a dust cloud, sending some of your carefully weighed ingredients up into the air.)

Creaming

When creaming butter and sugar, it should be done for a good length of time — 5 minutes or more — until the mixture is really light and fluffy. It is almost impossible to beat the mixture too much at this stage. However, once the flour is added, beat as little as possible, gently folding or stirring it in until just incorporated, as overbeating the mixture at this point will result in the cake being dense or heavy.

Adding liquid ingredients

When adding liquid ingredients to a cake batter, it is usually best to do this in a couple of batches, pouring in just a bit at a time and mixing well between each addition to properly combine the ingredients. Our sponge batter can be quite runny and may sometimes look a little split, but don't worry — your cake will still turn out beautifully.

Cooking times

These can really vary depending on your oven (and also how many items are baking at the same time). Just because the specified cooking time is up, it doesn't automatically mean the cake is done. For every recipe, we give a time range, so use this as a rough guide, checking your cake after the minimum time, but leaving it for longer if it needs more time in the oven, and checking it regularly. Try to avoid opening the oven door until the minimum recommended cooking time, or you risk your sponge sinking.

Testing when cooked

To tell when your cake is ready, insert a skewer into the middle of it. If it comes out clean, with no mixture stuck to it, the cake is cooked. You should also look to see if it is well risen, springy on top and golden brown (though this last bit obviously depends on the flavour or colour of the cake — for example, a chocolate sponge will never be golden!).

Cooling

Cakes should be completely cool before you frost or store them. The frosting might melt or slide off the cake otherwise, or the cupcake cases may peel away too readily.

Frosting Cupcakes

1. Use a 50ml (1¾fl oz) ice-cream scoop, if you have one, to place a generous amount of frosting on top of the cupcake. These can be bought online and are sometimes known as food-portioners.

2. With the flat surface of a palette knife, spread the frosting around the top of the cake, smoothing downwards and making sure it covers all the way to the edge of the paper case.

3. Put the flat tip of the palette knife in the centre and move in a circular motion to make an indented swirl in the frosting.

4. To create a pretty peak on top, lift the palette knife upwards at the last second.

5. Now enjoy your gorgeous Hummingbird cupcake with its perfect swirled frosting. If you wish, sprinkle over the decoration of your choice, such as coloured strands.

Frosting Layer Cakes

1. Place the first layer of sponge on a board or plate. With a palette knife, smooth a generous amount of frosting onto the sponge, making sure it is evenly spread and almost reaches the edges. Place the second sponge layer on top and smooth on the frosting as you did for the first layer.

2. Add the third sponge layer in the same way. (If you're making a four-layer cake, the third sponge layer will need to be topped with frosting and the fourth layer added too.) Then lightly frost the sides of the cake. This is just a 'base coat' to pick up any loose crumbs. Also give the top of the cake a light base coat of frosting.

3. Now frost the sides and the top of the cake again, this time with a thicker layer of frosting; it should be thick enough that you can't see any of the sponge through the frosting.

4. Using the flat tip of the palette knife, add texture to the sides of the cake by either gently pulling the palette knife upwards, from bottom to top, to create lines in the frosting or by pulling the palette knife around the circumference of the cake to create the lines.

5. Again using the flat tip of the palette knife, create the pattern on the top of the cake by starting from the outside edge and pulling the knife over the frosting and into the middle in gentle curved lines.

Index

A

Alabama Little Layer Cake 78–81

Ambrosia Cookies 120–1

American Flaky Pastry, Basic 92

Appalachian Stack Cake 87–9

apples:

Apple Bread Pudding 220–1

Deep-fried Apple Pies 100–1

Kentucky Apple Pancake
184–5

B

bacon: Peanut Butter Chocolate
Banana Bacon Pie 102–3

bananas:

Bananas Foster Bread
Pudding 214–15

Bananas Foster Cupcakes
39–41

Peanut Butter Chocolate Banana
Bacon Pie 102–3

bars:

Blackberry Limeade Bars 162–3

Caramel Chocolate Chip
Cookie Bars 160–1

Coconut Dream Bars 154–5

Pumpkin Hazelnut Bars 158–9

Texas Tassie Bars 164–5

Beignets, New Orleans 242–3

Birthday Cake Cookies 140–1

biscuits:

Buttermilk Biscuits 226–7

Sweet Potato Biscuits 240–1

Black and White Cookies 128–30

Black Bottom Pancakes 174–5

Black Fruitcake 16–17

Black Pepper Cookies 126–7

blackberries:

Blackberry Limeade Bars 162–3

Blackberry Sonker 108–9

Blue Hawaiian Cupcakes 36–8

Blueberry Cream Cheese Pie
104–5

bourbon 247

Bourbon Bread Pudding 212–13

Kentucky Bourbon Cake 20–1

bread & savouries 224–45

Buttermilk Biscuits 226–7

Cinnamon Raisin Swirl Loaf
238–9

Crawfish Pie 234–5

Graham Crackers 244–5

New Orleans Beignets 242–3

Pumpkin Crumb Muffins 236–7

Sally Lunn Loaf 228–9

Skillet Cornbread 230–1

Sweet Potato Biscuits 240–1

Sweet Potato Cornbread 232–3

bread pudding:

Apple Bread Pudding 220–1

Bananas Foster Bread Pudding
214–15

Bourbon Bread Pudding 212–13

Praline Bread Pudding with Pecan
Caramel Sauce 216–17

White Chocolate Bread Pudding
222

brownies:

Brownie Pudding 218–19

Chocolate Carrot Brownies
166–7

Red Velvet Brownies 156–7

Bundt Cake, Chocolate 22–3

Butter Cake, Gooey 10–11

buttermilk 246

Buttermilk Biscuits 226–7

Buttermilk Ice Cream 190–1

Buttermilk Pancakes 176–7

C

cakes, single 9–31

Black Fruitcake 16–17

Chocolate Bundt Cake 22–3

Gingerbread Cake 26–7

Gooey Butter Cake 10–11

Kentucky Bourbon Cake 20–1

Molasses Pecan Crumb Cake
18–19

Oatmeal Spice Cake 12–13

Ozark Pudding Cake 24–5

7Up Pound Cake 14–15

Tunnel of Fudge Cake 28–9

Upside-down Pear Cake 30–1

caramel:

Caramel Chocolate Chip
Cookie Bars 160–1

Praline Bread Pudding with
Pecan Caramel Sauce 216–17

Pumpkin Caramels 144–5

Carrot Chocolate Brownies 166–7

Chai Cupcakes, Pumpkin 42–3

chiffon pie:

Lemon Chiffon Pie 96–7

Strawberry Chiffon Pie 93–5

chocolate:

Caramel Chocolate Chip
Cookie Bars 160–1

Chocolate Bundt Cake 22–3

Chocolate Carrot Brownies
166–7

Chocolate Chip 'Cupcakes' 52–3

Chocolate Doberge Cake 62–5

Earl Grey Tea and Chocolate
Ice Cream 200–1

German Chocolate Cake 72–3

Peanut Butter Chocolate Banana
Bacon Pie 102–3

Pumpkin and White Chocolate

Cookies 136–7
Vanilla-filled Chocolate Cookies
131–3
White Chocolate Bread Pudding
222
cinnamon:
Cinnamon Pancake Cake 182–3
Cinnamon Raisin Swirl Loaf
238–9
Coconut Dream Bars 154–5
cookies & candies 118–49
Ambrosia Cookies 120–1
Birthday Cake Cookies 140–1
Black and White Cookies 128–30
Black Pepper Cookies 126–7
Cornmeal Cookies 134–5
Creamy Pecan Pralines 146–7
Divinity 148–9
Lemon Drops 138–9
Peanut Butter and Marshmallow
Cookies 124–5
Pumpkin and White Chocolate
Cookies 136–7
Pumpkin Caramels 144–5
Soft Molasses Cookies 122–3
Turtle Cookies 142–3
Vanilla-filled Chocolate Cookies
131–3
Cookie Bars, Caramel Chocolate
Chip 160–1
cornbread:
Honey Cornbread Cupcakes
54–5
Skillet Cornbread 230–1
Sweet Potato Cornbread 232–3
Cornmeal Cookies 134–5
Crackers, Graham 244–5
Crawfish Pie 234–5
Cream Cheese Pie, Blueberry
104–5
Crepe Cake, Red Velvet 84–6

cupcakes 32–57
Bananas Foster Cupcakes 39–41
Blue Hawaiian Cupcakes 36–8
Chocolate Chip 'Cupcakes' 52–3
frosting 250
Grape Jelly Cupcakes 34–5
Honey Cornbread Cupcakes 54–5
Mint Julep Cupcakes 56–7
Pink Champagne Cupcakes 46–9
Pumpkin Chai Cupcakes 42–3
Toasted Marshmallow Cupcakes
50–1
Tomato Soup Cupcakes 44–5
Custard Ice Cream, Lemon
208–9

D
Divinity 148–9
doberge cake:
Chocolate Doberge Cake 62–5
Lemon Doberge Cake 74–7

E
Earl Grey tea:
Earl Grey Tea and Chocolate
Ice Cream 200–1
Earl Grey Tea Pie 112–13
equipment 248

F
Fig Ice Cream, South Carolina
202–3
Flaky Pastry, Basic American 92
French Toast, Sally Lunn 186–7
frosting 250–1
Fruitcake, Black 16–17
Fudge Cake, Tunnel of 28–9

G
German Chocolate Cake 72–3
gingerbread:
Gingerbread Cake 26–7

Gingerbread Icebox Cake 69–71
Gooey Butter Cake 10–11
Graham Crackers 244–5
Grape Jelly Cupcakes 34–5
Grasshopper Pie Ice Cream 196–7

H
Hasty Pudding 223
Hawaiian Cupcakes, Blue 36–8
hazelnut:
Hazelnut Pumpkin Bars 158–9
Honey Cornbread Cupcakes 54–5

I
Icebox Pie, Piña Colada 114–15
Icebox Cake, Gingerbread 69–71
ice cream 188–209, 248
Buttermilk Ice Cream 190–1
Earl Grey Tea and Chocolate
Ice Cream 200–1
Fresh Peach Ice Cream 204–5
Grasshopper Pie Ice Cream 196–7
Lemon Custard Ice Cream 208–9
Peanut Butter Ice Cream 206–7
Pumpkin Ice Cream 198–9
Red Velvet Ice Cream 192–5
South Carolina Fig Ice Cream
202–3
ice-cream makers 248
ingredients 246–7

J
jelly:
Grape Jelly Cupcakes 34–5
Peanut Butter and Jelly Cake
60–1

K
Kentucky Apple Pancake 184–5
Kentucky Bourbon Cake 20–1

L

Lady Baltimore Cake 66–8

layer cakes 58–89

    Alabama Little Layer Cake 78–81

    Appalachian Stack Cake 87–9

    Chocolate Doberge Cake 62–5

    frosting 250

    German Chocolate Cake 72–3

    Gingerbread Icebox Cake 69–71

    Lady Baltimore Cake 66–8

    Lemon Doberge Cake 74–7

    Orange Layer Cake 82–3

    Peanut Butter and Jelly Cake 60–1

    Red Velvet Crepe Cake 84–6

lemon:

    Lemon Chiffon Pie 96–7

    Lemon Crumb Squares 152–3

    Lemon Custard Ice Cream
      208–9

    Lemon Drops 138–9

    Lemon Doberge Cake 74–7

    Shaker Lemon Pie 98–9

Limeade Bars, Blackberry 162–3

Little Layer Cake, Alabama 78–81

loaves:

    Cinnamon Raisin Swirl Loaf
      238–9

    Sally Lunn Loaf 228–9

M

marshmallow:

    Toasted Marshmallow Cupcakes
      50–1

    Peanut Butter and Marshmallow
      Cookies 124–5

methods & techniques 249–50

Mint Julep Cupcakes 56–7

molasses 247

    Molasses Pecan Crumb Cake
      18–19

    Soft Molasses Cookies 122–3

Muffins, Pumpkin Crumb 236–7

O

oatmeal:

    Oatmeal Pancakes 180–1

    Oatmeal Spice Cake 12–13

Orange Layer Cake 82–3

Ozark Pudding Cake 24–5

P

pancakes 170–87

    Black Bottom Pancakes 174–5

    Buttermilk Pancakes 176–7

    Cinnamon Pancake Cake 182–3

    Kentucky Apple Pancake 184–5

    Oatmeal Pancakes 180–1

    Pumpkin Pancakes 178–9

    Red Velvet Pancakes 172–3

Pastry, Basic American Flaky 92

Peach Ice Cream, Fresh 204–5

peanut butter:

    Peanut Butter and Jelly Cake
      60–1

    Peanut Butter and Marshmallow
      Cookies 124–5

    Peanut Butter Chocolate Banana
      Bacon Pie 102–3

    Peanut Butter Ice Cream 206–7

pear:

    Pear Treasure Squares 168–9

    Upside-down Pear Cake 30–1

pecan:

    Creamy Pecan Pralines 146–7

    Molasses Pecan Crumb Cake 18–19

    Praline Bread Pudding with
      Pecan Caramel Sauce 216–17

pies 90–117

    Basic American Flaky Pastry 92

    Blackberry Sonker 108–9

    Blueberry Cream Cheese Pie
      104–5

    Deep-fried Apple Pies 100–1

    Earl Grey Tea Pie 112–13

    Lemon Chiffon Pie 96–7

    New Orleans Prune Pie 116–17

    Peanut Butter Chocolate Banana
      Bacon Pie 102–3

    Piña Colada Icebox Pie 114–15

    Shaker Lemon Pie 98–9

    Sliced Sweet Potato Pie 106–7

    Strawberry Chiffon Pie 93–5

    Vinegar Pie 110–11

Piña Colada Icebox Pie 114–15

Pink Champagne Cupcakes 46–9

potato *see* Sweet Potato

Pound Cake, 7Up 14–15

praline:

    Creamy Pecan Pralines 146–7

    Praline Bread Pudding with
      Pecan Caramel Sauce 216–17

Prune Pie, New Orleans 116–17

puddings 210–23

    Apple Bread Pudding 220–1

    Bananas Foster Bread Pudding
      214–15

    Bourbon Bread Pudding 212–13

    Brownie Pudding 218–19

    Hasty Pudding 223

    Ozark Pudding Cake 24–5

    Praline Bread Pudding with
      Pecan Caramel Sauce 216–17

    White Chocolate Bread Pudding
      222

pumpkin 247

    Pumpkin and White Chocolate
      Cookies 136–7

    Pumpkin Caramels 144–5

    Pumpkin Chai Cupcakes 42–3

    Pumpkin Crumb Muffins 236–7

    Pumpkin Hazelnut Bars 158–9

    Pumpkin Ice Cream 198–9

    Pumpkin Pancakes 178–9

R

Raisin Swirl Loaf, Cinnamon 238–9

red velvet:

Red Velvet Brownies 156–7
Red Velvet Crepe Cake 84–6
Red Velvet Ice Cream 192–5
Red Velvet Pancakes 172–3

S
Sally Lunn:
Sally Lunn French Toast 186–7
Sally Lunn Loaf 228–9
7Up Pound Cake 14–15
Shaker Lemon Pie 98–9
Skillet Cornbread 230–1
Sonker, Blackberry 108–9
Soup Cupcakes, Tomato 44–5
South Carolina Fig Ice Cream 202–3
Spice Cake, Oatmeal 12–13
Stack Cake, Appalachian 87–9
Strawberry Chiffon Pie 93–5
sweet potato:
Sliced Sweet Potato Pie 106–7
Sweet Potato Biscuits 240–1
Sweet Potato Cornbread 232–3
Swirl Loaf, Cinnamon Raisin 238–9

T
Tea Pie, Earl Grey 112–13
Texas Tassie Bars 164–5
Toasted Marshmallow Cupcakes
50–1
Tomato Soup Cupcakes 44–5
traybakes 150–69
Blackberry Limeade Bars 162–3
Caramel Chocolate Chip Cookie
Bars 160–1
Chocolate Carrot Brownies
166–7
Coconut Dream Bars 154–5
Lemon Crumb Squares 152–3
Pear Treasure Squares 168–9
Pumpkin Hazelnut Bars 158–9
Red Velvet Brownies 156–7
Texas Tassie Bars 164–5
Treasure Squares, Pear 168–9

Tunnel of Fudge Cake 28–9
Turtle Cookies 142–3

U
Upside-down Pear Cake 30–1

V
Vanilla-filled Chocolate Cookies
131–3
Vinegar Pie 110–11

Acknowledgements

I would like to thank my mother, Hanan Malouf, and my sister, Juman Malouf, for encouraging me to write this book and for showing me that finding inspiration for sweet treats could come by travelling, exploring and keeping my eyes open even in the strangest of places. A double thank you to Hanan for accompanying me on my trip to the USA and eating everything put on the plate in front of her in the name of research!

Visiting the South would not have been as much fun or as tasty if it weren't for the following people: my aunt Dr Najla Malouf, and my cousins Ruth and Mike McGranahan in Durham, North Carolina; my cousins Bert and Amy Anderson in Atlanta; Beth Jones Nazar in New Orleans, my friend of over 25 years; and Christi McCrary in Dallas, who I've known since we were 14 years old and who took me to the Texas State Fair to eat a deep-fried peanut butter, banana and jelly sandwich.

Thank you to Zoë Waldie for your on-going support and guidance – and for taking care of my mother now that Deborah has gone.

Thank you to Louise Haines and Georgia Mason at Fourth Estate for taking me in so warmly and for being excited about my mad recipes.

A big thank you to Joss Herd and Bianca Nice for testing everything so wonderfully and enthusiastically and faithfully, no matter how bizarre the ingredient or how gigantic the end product. Thank you to Myfanwy Vernon-Hunt for continuing to make things gorgeous and feel just perfectly Hummingbird; and to Kate Whitaker, working with you on the past three books has been a privilege, and more beautiful each time.

And a final thank you to my wonderful colleagues, past, present and future, at The Hummingbird Bakery – I continue to be lucky to have you.

Fourth Estate
An imprint of HarperCollins*Publishers*
1 London Bridge Street
London, SE1 9GF
www.4thestate.co.uk

First published in Great Britain
by Fourth Estate 2015

A catalogue record for this book is available from the British Library

ISBN 978-0-00-756459-0

Printed and bound in China by South China Printing Co Ltd.